Core Resource

EDUCATION AND INCOME

In republican schools, there must be no temptation to the growth of aristocratical prejudices. The pupils must learn to consider themselves as fellow citizens, as equals. Respect ought to be paid, and will always be paid, to virtue and talent; but it ought not to be paid to riches, or withheld from poverty. Yet, if the children from these state schools are to go every evening, the one to his wealthy parent's soft carpeted drawing room, and the other to its poor father's or widowed mother's comfortless cabin, will they return the next day as friends and equals? He knows little of human nature who thinks they will.

—Robert Dale Owen

Education and Income

INEQUALITIES OF OPPORTUNITY
IN OUR PUBLIC SCHOOLS

Patricia Cayo Sexton

Assistant Professor
of Educational Sociology, New York University

FOREWORD BY Kenneth B. Clark

Professor of Psychology,
College of the City of New York

 THE VIKING PRESS NEW YORK 1961

FIRST PUBLISHED IN 1961 BY THE VIKING PRESS, INC.
625 MADISON AVENUE, NEW YORK 22, N.Y.

PUBLISHED SIMULTANEOUSLY IN CANADA BY
THE MACMILLAN COMPANY OF CANADA LIMITED

SECOND PRINTING OCTOBER 1962

LIBRARY OF CONGRESS CATALOG CARD NUMBER: 61-10446

PRINTED IN THE U.S.A. BY THE VAIL-BALLOU PRESS

*To Alice and Brendan
with love*

ACKNOWLEDGMENTS

The responsibility for conducting this study and writing this book is mine, but so much of what is in it has emerged from long and continuing conversations with my husband, Brendan Sexton, a number of the key ideas originating with him as well as most of the inspiration, that I feel this work is almost a collaboration, in plan if not in execution.

With deep indebtedness to: Arthur Kornhauser and Mary Kornhauser for their warm encouragement, careful reading of the manuscript, and dozens of editorial suggestions, most of which were put to use; Guy Nunn for his continuing and unobtrusive assistance and kindness; Vera Dunham for several vital pieces of friendly advice; Eleanor Wolfe for help during critical moments; Edgar Johnston, August Kerber, Mildred Peters, Mel Ravitz for assistance throughout a difficult project; Charles Bolté and Denver Lindley for help given beyond the call of duty; Marvin Bressler for much ex post facto aid. The assistance has been all the more generous since in some cases it has been given despite disagreement with the author's point of view.

Foreword

The relationship between social class and education has deep historical roots. In the modern world, education itself has become one of the clearer symbols of prestige and status. The democratic revolution that was the founding and expansion of the United States of America attempted to repair historical inequities by offering education to the masses of the people, without regard to family position or wealth. A major promise of this new society, born of a literal belief in the equality of mankind, was the attempt to make education and schools the chief agent of social mobility, a means of self-improvement available to all.

Like all social experiments, this one has not always borne the expected fruits. In general, however, the American goal of an education not limited to the privileged classes has produced more good results than bad. The stream of immigrants who came to America in the nineteenth and early twentieth centuries came not only in search of economic success for themselves but also in urgent quest for better educational opportunities for their children. An important part of the American dream and promise was that low social or economic status of parents would not be a serious barrier to the education of any child of adequate intelligence. In the past this promise often seemed justified by the dramatic examples of those who rose from "rags to riches"—the Horatio Algers who emerged in one or two generations.

Within the past two decades a number of serious observers have become concerned at the increasing indications that the American public educational system, more efficient and elaborate than ever, has paradoxically become *less* effective as an instrument of social mobility. In fact, some have suggested that certain practices in American public schools have resulted in consolidating and intensifying distinctions among social classes. So far, these observers have had to depend for the most part on general observations, theoretical interpretations, and essentially value-oriented speculations as the basis for their criticisms. Almost the only empirical evidence in support of these criticisms came from an examination and comparison of the differences between the education provided for white children and that provided for Negro children in segregated schools. This type of evidence has been conclusive in pointing to intolerable inferiority in the quality of education provided for Negro children. The clarity of this evidence, however, tended to obscure the equally important problem of discrepancies in the quality of public-school education based upon social and class distinctions.

Dr. Sexton's study, reported in this book, is a significant contribution to this new and important dimension of the present discussions. She has presented concrete evidence which demonstrates beyond any reasonable doubt that our public-school system has rejected its role of facilitating social mobility and has become in fact an instrument of social and economic class distinctions in American society. Her evidence, obtained from the study of a single large, Northern, urban public-school system, is strong and cannot be ignored or explained away. This evidence must be examined by responsible educators, intelligent laymen, and those who have the power and authority to make the decisions which affect the lives of the people. To ignore this type of evidence would be tantamount to social irresponsibility at least—and criminal negligence at worst. This type of evidence must be used as the basis for serious, extensive re-examination of the American public-school system. Further evidence of this type must be obtained, analyzed, and used as the basis for the prompt development of a stable, practical, economical, and meaningful educational program, if our public schools are to fulfill their positive role in strengthening and expanding American democracy.

At this point in the history of America and of the world, America cannot afford to waste any of its human intellectual potential on such arbitrary and irrelevant grounds as race or social-class distinctions.

—Kenneth B. Clark

Contents

Foreword by Kenneth B. Clark   vii

Introduction   xiii

1. BIG CITY   1

    Big City Schools   5
    Objectivity   9
    Social Class and Income   10
    Education and Income: A National Picture   13
    The Race Question   15
    Planning the Study   18

2. ELEMENTARY SCHOOLS   21

    Success or Failure   25
    The Child and Environs   87
    The Parent   106
    The Quality of Education   113

3. LIFE AT HOME   137

    Community Problems   141

Parks and Recreation Areas   143
Experiences of Children   144

4. SENIOR HIGH SCHOOLS   149

Achievement Tests   155
In and Out of School   157
Success—Failure   159
After-School Groups   165
The Selecting and Sorting Process   171
The Quality of Education   211
Which Income Group Is Worst Off?   222

5. CONTROL OF THE SCHOOLS   225

Parents   227
Teachers   229
School Boards   234
A Fourth Force   238

6. UP TO DATE   239

Big City   241
New York City   242
The Great Cities Project   246
Britain   247

7. COMMENTS AND SUGGESTIONS   251

Finances   253
Curriculum   256
Further Research   275
Open Records   282
Experimental Programs   283

Notes   289

Index   294

Introduction

Much of the debate over education today, no matter how distantly related it may sometimes appear, can be reduced to a simple contest between "mass" and "elite" education. The debate began in this country when the first school was built and has continued unabated to the present moment.

As we look back, it seems clear that, in the past, educational advantages have gone to those who could pay the price—to an elite of wealth, in other words. Education has not always been free. Advanced education has always been costly. Money has been needed to purchase it. Thus the elite of wealth and the elite of the educated were usually identical.

Today the situation is not so simple. Education through high school in most places is now free—at least for those who can afford the hidden tuition charges and the expense of unemployment.

Higher education is still very costly, yet scholarships are now available for the poor but able.

Our educated elite has expanded and now includes a

number of those who came up the hard way, through the ranks.

Many assume from these facts that an elite of ability, rather than an elite of wealth, is receiving most of the educational advantages we now offer. They are pleased by this arrangement, and they are content that our schools are doing a good job of educating an ability elite.

Some, however, question the relationship of "ability" with the old categories of wealth and status. Jacques Barzun in *The House of Intellect* calls attention to the unearned advantage of ancestry and of being born to the elite: "There is no mystery about it: the child who is familiar with books, ideas, conversation—the ways and means of the intellectual life—before he begins school, indeed, before he begins consciously to think, has a marked advantage. He is at home in the House of Intellect just as the stableboy is at home among horses or the child of actors on the stage. Medical schools recognize this truth when they give preference to applicants who are children of physicians."

Yet, strangely, he would not have the elite of wealth and status wait in line with the elite of ability. The old elite must go to the head of the line: "If we remember . . . how frequently talent is born into families with developed intellectual interests, it is at once obvious that the children of such families should be given preference. Their 'need' is of a different order from that of the ordinary good student. Besides, such families are doubtless more prosperous than the average, they have more expensive tastes, and they will want to send not one, but all their children, to college. And it should be one of the best colleges."

Admiral Rickover, on the other hand, argues for a more rigidly administered system of ability grouping. The one

we have now, he feels, is too imperfect. Faced with the threat
of Soviet educational superiority, we need, he feels, to put
all our resources into the education of an ability elite. His
complaints about our system are: We are trying to educate
a great many students who are not able to learn; some of
those who *are* able to learn cannot afford to stay in school;
and—most important in his schema—students with "ability" should be segregated from the less able and given special preferred treatment.

Our basic educational error, he feels, was the comprehensive high school, a school which brought together under
the same roof, though often in different curriculums, students of diverse abilities and from all levels of society.

Those responsible for this grave error did not know, he
claims, that "aptitude for learning above the elementary
level was relatively rare." To correct this error, we must
segregate the gifted from the masses, much as officers are
separated from the men, and we must give them training
worthy of an intellectual elite. And the others, the masses?
He does not specify what their fate should be, but it is clear
he does not think they can contribute much intellectually
or that they have any notable amounts of that "rare" aptitude for learning.

The admiral's views are shared by a great many current
critics of education. He holds these views despite his verbal
recognition that the Soviets, whose educational superiority
he fears, seem to excel at "mass" education and that we will
have to run to keep up with their educational accomplish-
ments.

He does not recall, apparently, that, though Soviet
schools are as authoritarian as military academies, they do
not separate the "gifted" from the ranks, their high schools

are "comprehensive," they do not give IQ tests, and they *claim* at least that intellect is much more a product of circumstances than of birth. What is more, in admission to college they give some degree of preference to students coming up from the ranks, even though they may seem less able than others.

Keeping up with the Soviets is not the only problem with education designed almost exclusively for an ability elite.

Robert Owen saw some of the other problems. Though Owen paid his respects to those possessing "virtue and talent," he did not go overboard for an ability elite. He saw what many critics of education cannot see: that elite groups, even when selected by the most rigorous tests of "merit and ability" derive their status much more from their "rich carpeted drawing rooms" and from accidents of environment and association than from superior virtue or talent.

Owen made these observations in the highly stratified society of 1830; yet what he saw can be seen just as clearly today, everywhere, in the richest democracy of all time as well as in the settled societies of the Old World.

The system has not changed much; it has simply changed form with a rising standard of living for people at all levels and ranks.

The doors of opportunity have been opened, but not very wide. Those who pass through first are simply newer generations of the same groups who came first in Owen's day. Mostly they are members of the old elites of wealth and status, disguised now as an elite of ability. Others of course pass through before the doors close, but their numbers are small considering the size of the crowd that is left waiting.

In the schools of modern America we still find that children from "comfortless cabins" or, to shift time and locale, from "urban slums" cannot compete with the children of the elite. This is true not necessarily because of any deficiency of talent or ability but because society, being dominated by elites, has given their children a head start and, following the lead as always, the schools have compounded the advantage by providing them with superior educational services of every conceivable variety.

Slum children and Southern Negroes, victims of segregated education and inferior schools, are not the only ones to incur a disadvantage in this arrangement. Everyone in a stratified society incurs a disadvantage, the weight of the handicap decreasing with the approach to the summit.

Negroes of course, both in the South and in the North, bear the heaviest burden of inequities, but they do not suffer alone. Everyone suffers—some much more than others.

Now accumulating evidence shows that even when children from the lower ranks manage somehow to break through despite their handicaps, when they somehow "score" on the tests of "talent and ability" which have been set up to screen them out—even then they often do not make the grade.

So it is that 50 per cent of the "top" 10 per cent of high-school graduates do not go to college. Apparently many of these students know their place, and that place is more likely to be found on an assembly line than in a college. They cannot afford college very often, and they do not feel they "belong" there. Moreover, since they have often been denied, by accident or intention, all information about the mechanics of selecting a college, being admitted, applying for scholarships or financial aid, etc., they would not know how to go even if they were able and willing.

Painful as it may be to face, estimates are that the worker's child in the USSR has *twice* as good a chance of going to college as his US counterpart (*Harvard Educational Review*, Spring 1957)—an ugly fact, but one we must permit to crawl out from under its rock. Only then can we see the size and shape of the adversary.

Of course, in this country an occasional slum child may find his way into a state university, and some will point to this as evidence of equal educational opportunity. Chances are very good, however, that the rare slum child who is admitted to the state university will flunk out in his first semester—without the university's raising a finger to help him with his academic difficulties or noticing his presence or his absence once he is gone. With luck the slum child may manage to hang on in college. When he does, he may finish teachers' college or the school of social work, and with his degree move up into the ranks of the lowest-paid professionals in the field. If this happens, he will be among the relatively few lucky ones in his class.

In a society with an ever-growing demand for high-level skills and a rapidly decreasing demand for unskilled labor, the failure of students who are top-ranking in scores but low-ranking in privileges to go on to college is a grievous loss. But the problem is much bigger than this. Paying respect to riches or status and withholding it from poverty, in either overt or subtle ways, has much more serious consequences in a democratic industrial society than the simple denial of higher education to the less privileged, however great the loss of "talent" may be.

An industrial society, if it is to grow at top speed, as ours must, should call on the full intellectual potential of *all* the people in that society—not just those in Rickover's ability elite. It must, in other words, engage in all-out mass education, with full equality of opportunity extended to all students. This our nation has failed to do.

The "ground swell" for learning has not yet emerged in our country, and under present conditions may never emerge. The knowledge, understanding, and participation required to reach democratic goals with efficiency, and the skills required for peak industrial performance, remain in very large part latent and undeveloped. We are not putting all our power into the nation's democratic and industrial effort. Though we have discovered how to release energy from the atom by fission and fusion, we have not yet discovered how to release the great untapped power of the average human mind, a power which in its collectivity might create miracles reaching far beyond hydrogen fusion.

Mass education, to be effective, will have to consider the handicaps of the underprivileged and the culturally deprived. It will have to take into account that the boy whose father works on an assembly line is less likely to have books in his home or to know anything about how to get into college than is the boy whose father is a college graduate. These things must be considered and some system of compensation must be worked out to deal with them.

The tools of effective mass education will probably be very different from those of old-style elite education. The approach will be different; the content, the method, the standards will perhaps all be different. The tools of elite education, as has been demonstrated through the years, apparently cannot do the job of enlisting the full resources and the full participation of the majority in intellectual pursuits. Let us face it, unpleasant though it may be: Ours is not a nation which has been very seriously interested in

developing the riches and resources of the mind. One does
not have to look very deeply to see that most people have
little interest in our schools, that what is provided in the
mass media seems often to be an escape from learning, and
that anti-egghead sentiment appears to be the prevailing
reaction to "intellectualism" in our country.

The problem seems to demand a new style of education,
a style which will evoke the interest and participation,
rather than the indifference and hostility, of the majority
group.

Perhaps with this new approach we can have *real* mass
education in our nation. And perhaps then we can mount
an educational assault which will be democratic and at the
same time effectively competitive with Soviet authoritarian
education. Through mass education, perhaps we can break
down some of the walls of class and status described in these
pages, walls which seem totally out of place in a democratic
egalitarian society such as we want ours to be. With the re-
moval of these barriers, perhaps we can make a closer approach to the greatest of all democratic dreams—equal educational opportunity for all, without regard to race, reli-
gion, class, or status.

This is the Dream.

The exploration in the following pages of school inequalities, social class distinctions, and the relation between
income and educational opportunity—as seen particularly
in Big City schools—is the Reality.

This is the first *study* of its kind. One of the barriers to
such research in the past has been the refusal of school administrators to give out information of the type included
here. Such data, they claim, is too sensitive for the general
public ear. Moreover, information on individual schools,

they say, permits invidious comparisons between schools.

The present exploration might not have been permitted had it not been for a recent change in top administration in Big City. The new superintendent of schools was interested in getting the schools and the community together.

One of his first acts was to set up a citizens' committee on school needs. Since then, he has made continuing efforts to open up the schools to public examination, and though the current study did not seem warmly welcomed, it was not rejected out of hand. In previous years, it probably would have been.

It is certainly not claimed that there is *no* interest in the problems discussed here. On the contrary, there are a number of concerned people in the schools and in the community who have thought about the problems, and some who have made heroic efforts to do something about them.

Yet, considering the size and urgency of the problems, the number of interested parties has been appallingly small to date, and research on many of these vital matters has been meager and often nonexistent.

Though a dozen books and over five hundred articles have been written in the recent past about the problems of the "gifted" child, not a single major work and only a scattering of articles have dealt with the special problems of the "average" child, the culturally deprived, or with matters of social class inequalities in the schools.

The present study is an attempt to break through the barrier of inertia, indifference, and opposition to an understanding of the Reality of our schools and our society.

Perhaps America's most challenging job is to make this Reality measure up to our great national Dream.

1

Big City

Humanly speaking, the school, the college,
society, make the difference between men.
—Ralph Waldo Emerson

BIG CITY

Bıg City is located in midwest America.

It is one of the largest cities in the country and by many standards the most prosperous. In retail sales per family in 1957 Big City ranked highest among the five largest cities in the nation. In the same year the median family income in the greater city area was $6200—$1200 above the national median.

Strictly within the city limits the median family income was $5600, meaning that half of all families in the city made less and half made more than $5600. The *average* family income was much higher—$6900.

These income levels are unusually high because Big City is an industrial area and its industrial workers are well paid, even those who are unskilled and inexperienced.

Also, except for recessions, which always hit Big City very hard, there has been a high level of employment in the city, with wives and other normally dependent persons working and some eager wage-earners holding down more than one job.

Because of high wage and employment levels, Big City has offered more opportunities and a better living standard to lower-income groups than most other cities. In 1958, despite a severe recession which struck Big City harder than it did any other major city, only 22 per cent of all families in the metropolitan area earned less than $4000. The comparable figure in New York was 23 per cent and in Chicago 25 per cent. So, badly off as lower-income groups in Big City may seem to be, they are better off than comparable groups in other cities.

Like most urban areas, Big City has tended to develop in concentric circles, the older residents moving farther away from the center of the city with increasing prosperity, and new unskilled migrants moving into the downtown and central areas. Because of this pattern of movement, people of similar incomes tend to be clustered together in the city, the lowest-income groups in the central areas, with income generally increasing with distance from the center of town.

There are almost no areas in the city where one can find, as in Manhattan, a plush apartment building right alongside slum housing. In Big City—unlike New York, Chicago, San Francisco, and the more urbane centers—upper-income groups live almost exclusively in the outskirts of town or in the suburbs; very few live in Gold Coast apartment developments in midtown. Median family income is therefore considerably higher in the suburbs ($7200) than within the city limits ($5600).

We shall not identify the city much further than this; it will not be necessary, for our purposes. Nor will we call the city by name—for two reasons. One: it seems to be contrary to the academic code to bite the hand that feeds you information. Two: naming it might focus too much attention on a single city, whereas our purpose is to direct attention to all cities.

Big City is quite typical of American cities. At any rate it is certainly much more typical than it is extraordinary. Except in some minor characteristics, a few of which we have mentioned, it could be taken for any of a number of cities throughout the country. Because of its many similarities with other cities of its size, we will simply use the generic name "Big City" as identification and let it go at that.

Big City Schools

The school system in Big City is also very much like school systems in other cities, as evidence from New York, Chicago, and other areas indicates.

Since schools do not appear to be much worse or much better than schools elsewhere, we shall not try to blame anyone for conditions found to exist in them. Such conditions are almost to be expected, since they appear to be merely a repetition of a nationwide pattern. Furthermore they result much more from neglect, indifference, and lack of understanding than from intention or malicious prejudice. However deplorable the social class system and the conditions in lower-income schools of Big City, there is no doubt that all people associated with the schools, perhaps without exception, would like students in lower-income schools to learn more and to have access to better facilities.

At the same time it appears that very few people with the power to alter the situation have concentrated any real attention on the problems of lower-income children or on the problems of stratification in the schools. Many who could or should have helped have given up in despair or exhaustion and moved on to easier educational problems. Many have not helped because they did not bother to acquaint themselves with the facts about a stratification system which makes it difficult for culturally *deprived* children to compete on equal terms with culturally *privileged* children.

Even more important, almost all educators, taking the easy way round this difficult and complicated problem, have put the blame for the educational failures of lower-income children on their "low IQ levels." And they have explained the school stratification system in terms of stratified IQ levels. According to this explanation, the child's inability to perform well in school is not the fault of the school, which may have neglected both him and his natural intellectual interests, nor is it the fault of a disturbed or inadequate home situation. The fault is with the child. "He is not very smart. The IQ tests prove that he isn't, so what can you do? The child simply can't learn more."

The truth about IQ scores, however, and about this easy explanation, is that there is no valid way of measuring native, inborn intelligence. In fact there isn't even agreement about what intelligence *is* or what the IQ tests should try to measure—but this is a matter for later discussion.

Another factor responsible for a school system in which lower-income children are neglected and rewards are given in almost direct proportion to family income levels is the belief, held by a surprisingly large number of people in and out of the schools, that preferential treatment *should* be given to upper-income groups and that so-called "gifted" children are worth much more than others. According to this view, the "gifted" (who come almost exclusively from upper-income groups, as this study shows) should be given better teachers, smaller classes, more and better school equipment—the best of everything available. In addition, it is argued, the main focus of the school's attention should be on the problems of these chosen ones.

Concerning the opposite end of the social class totem pole, this author has frequently heard teachers say in private that the "others," usually children from lower-income groups, aren't worth bothering much about and that the best you can do is keep them quiet and busy.

Such an unfortunate attitude seems to go with the general contempt these people often feel for their "social inferiors" and their preference for and desire to associate themselves with the "better" elements in the community. Certainly there is nothing in the situation or in the proven capacities of underprivileged children to indicate that they are "not worth bothering about."

In the final analysis, the neglect of lower-income students and the stratification system of the schools can probably be traced to three principal sources: one, the IQ evasion; two, the before-mentioned contempt, or at least indifference, which is often felt by teachers and others for their social "inferiors," and the irritation caused by their behavior, manners, and appearance; three, the fact that upper-income groups have usually been in control of school boards and thereby in control of what goes on in the schools and the methods of distributing rewards. In addition there is the fact that very little pressure is applied to the schools by lower-income individuals or groups representing them, while upper-income groups tend to have great influence in the schools and to be active in school affairs.

In a democratic society, schools must be committed to mass rather than to elite education. In carrying out this commitment, it would seem that the schools should aim to develop the full powers of *all* students, the "gifted" and the "others" alike.

Yet resistance to proposals for mass education and the premises on which they are based is great, perhaps because the stakes are so high. As the pioneer sociologist Lester Ward put it, "The proposition that the lower classes of society are the intellectual equals of the upper classes will probably shock most minds. At least it will be almost unanimously rejected as altogether false. . . .

"While the intellectually disinherited always include and are nearly coextensive with the materially disinherited, the former is much the more serious condition. For the intellectual inheritance would bring with it the material inheritance and all the other advantages that are enjoyed by the intelligent class.

"But here we encounter the great sullen, stubborn error, so universal and ingrained as to constitute a world view, that the difference between the upper and lower classes of society is due to a difference in their intellectual capacity, something existing in the nature of things, something preordained and inherently inevitable. Every form of sophistry is employed to uphold this view. . . .

"The difference in the native capacity of individuals is never sufficient to exclude any person from the highest social class. . . . It does not require any great or towering native abilities to enable an individual to maintain his place in the vanguard of society. The minimum natural abilities above the state of pathological imbecility suffice for this." [1]*

Objectivity

All researchers, being human and not mechanical, are involved with their subjects in one way or another. Everyone has preferences and a point of view. It is more honest, more scholarly, and less hypocritical to acknowledge the presence of sentiments. These sentiments, however, need not bias or divert the search for truth; in fact, under proper control they can serve to stimulate and motivate the search for truth.

We began this study with an acknowledged desire to help lower-income groups in school—if they needed help; this seemed to be a matter of elementary justice to which even the most indifferent would have to subscribe. We have subsequently looked at all available information about the schools in Big City. We have included in our study everything that could be considered relevant to the problems of social class in the schools, no matter what the data tended to prove about social class distinctions. Certainly school personnel, given their job involvements and their desire to "protect" certain sensitive information, could not have been more thorough or more impartial.

We have processed a mountain of material, and we have

* Numbered reference notes begin on page 289.

done the job as carefully and with as much deliberation as possible, motivated only by a compelling desire to learn the truth. This you will have to take our word for. If our findings tend to indicate rather overwhelmingly that social class distinctions *do* exist in Big City schools, we must insist that this is not attributable to our faulty or fixed vision, but to the way in which our schools and our society have been conducted.

Social Class and Income

The term "social class" has been defined in a number of ways. There are even those who deny that there is such a thing as social class in American life. The disputes about the legitimacy and the application of this term have been many and heated. We do not intend to enter into this dispute, though we can appreciate the ease with which we might slip into it unintentionally.

We will not argue about how rigid the social "classes" are in this country, how many there are, or how difficult it is to move from one to the other. Their number and rigidity varies from time to time and depends on the nation's prosperity, on technological advances, and on the changing political complexion of the country.

It cannot be denied, however, that children tend to be cast in the image of their parents. They learn their manners, their morals, their attitudes, their values—and much more—from their parents and families. They also learn how to make a living from them. A child whose father is an unskilled worker is also likely to become an unskilled worker. A child whose father is in business for himself will probably enter the business world too. This is what *we* mean by "social class," then: the position which families occupy in society and the very strong tendency for children to be molded into the same position by influences in the home, the community, and the school.

The home environment may handicap a child in school and in life, or it may be a source of special advantages. It may provide unusual opportunities or it may close all doors and shut out opportunity.

Family income is one index to social class, almost no matter how the term is defined. There are many other indices: occupation of father, type of housing, educational levels, etc. Family income is very highly correlated with all these other indices. Thus a "lower-class" family will tend to have a low income, lower-status (and lower-paying) occupations, poor housing, and low educational levels. A family possessing any one of these characteristics will tend to possess all of them.

There are exceptions, of course.

For example, some white-collar workers and some professionals (teachers, librarians, etc.) have rather low incomes compared with their educational levels. In general, however, income tends to increase with educational levels.

Of course the very highest levels of education are not necessarily the most materially rewarding, nor are the wealthiest the most likely to become scholars and intellectuals, but this is exceptional to the general pattern.

In Big City in 1957 income and education were related as shown in the first table on page 12.

In general, therefore, the more education the family head has, the higher the family income is likely to be. Between steps of this educational ladder, the greatest difference by a large margin ($1600) is found between the incomes of those who went to college and those who graduated only from high school.

EDUCATION (FAMILY HEAD)	MEDIAN FAMILY INCOME
6 years or less	$4700
7 to 8 years	5400
9 to 11 years	5800
Complete high school	6500
College	8100

In the same year family income was related to the "occupation" of the family head in the following way.

OCCUPATION (FAMILY HEAD)	MEDIAN FAMILY INCOME
Operatives, service workers	$5400
Clerical, sales workers	6300
Craftsmen, foremen	6900
Professionals, managers, proprietors, officials	8700

Between steps, the greatest difference by far ($1800) is found between the incomes of craftsmen and foremen on the one hand and professionals, etc., on the other.

The index also shows that white-collar workers (clerical and sales) are much better paid than unskilled and semi-skilled blue-collar workers (operatives and service). The difference in income is $900.

During periods of recession income differences between these two groups became even greater. The recession year of 1958 had a far greater impact on blue-collar than on white-collar workers in the city. During that year, because of lay-offs and reduced work weeks, the income of "operatives and service workers" declined $500 from the 1957 median. The incomes of "craftsmen and foremen" declined $200. At the same time the incomes of "clerical and sales workers" *increased* by $400. The incomes of "professionals" and kindred occupations increased by the same amount.

Thus, while in 1957 the difference between the incomes of white- and blue-collar workers was $900, in the recession year of 1958 it was $1800—exactly twice as much.

Not only was family income closely related to occupation and educational levels, it was also found that in Big City income had a correlation of .94 with the "socio-economic classification of community areas" (housing conditions, public assistance, behavior, vital data, as well as occupation and education). This very high correlation indicates that income is very intimately related to all social class characteristics and that it is therefore a good index to social class. We have used it as an index rather than other factors because we have found that, for our purposes, it is the simplest, most graphic, and most manageable of all the indicators of social class.

Education and Income: A National Picture

A national survey (1949) of earnings as they relate to educational levels produced the results shown in Figures 1 and 2.

National surveys show that job security also increases sharply with educational levels. A college graduate had almost twice as good a chance of working throughout the 1958 recession as did the person with only an elementary-school education.

The Survey Research Center of the University of Mich-

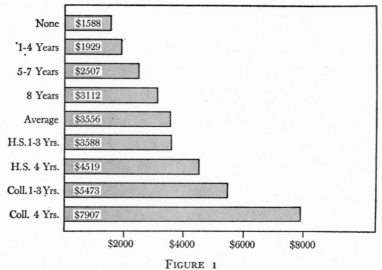

FIGURE 1
Average (mean) income of men 45 to 54 years old by
amount of education

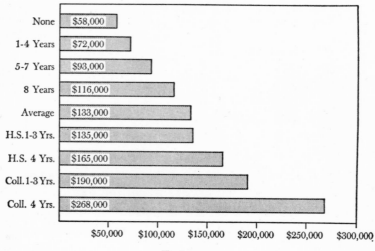

FIGURE 2
Estimated "lifetime" income for men by amount of education

igan found that a holder of a college degree had a 90 per cent chance of being employed for the full year, a high-school graduate had a 75 per cent chance, and a worker with less than nine years of formal education had only a 50 per cent chance.

According to this national survey, about one in six families falls into the low-income, low-education category. Almost two-thirds of those who earn incomes of less than $2000 annually have no more than an elementary-school education.

The problem will get worse for the unskilled and the uneducated. By 1970, it is predicted, about 45 per cent of all jobs in the country will be "white-collar." In the "professions," an increase of 60 per cent over the 1957 figure is expected by 1970.

The national demand for high-level skills is great, and the rewards, in income and security, are of comparable dimensions.

The Race Question

In Big City the income of Negroes is considerably lower than the income of whites. In 1957 Negro median family income was $4400—$2200 less than the income of whites.

In 1958 Negro income declined so sharply as a result of the recession that the difference amounted to $2600. Moreover, during the period 1951 through 1958, white income increased 31 per cent, while Negro income increased only 6 per cent.

Because of these depressed income levels, some people might claim that low-income groups do poorly in school because there are so many Negroes in them.

We have found, however, that, in low-income groups, students in predominantly Negro schools did just as well in school as, and were achieving at approximately equal levels with, students in predominantly white schools. The same thing was true in higher-income groups. In other areas of the country it has been found that Negroes perform somewhat better in school than whites with similar incomes.

The problems we describe, then, are principally social class problems, not racial problems. Of course the social class position of Negroes is generally much worse than that of whites and much more "frozen" by prejudice which limits their job opportunities and income levels, while providing inferior segregated education and housing in overcrowded, neglected ghetto areas. For Negroes the class system has almost the rigidity of a caste system, and indeed could accurately be called a semi-caste system. Restricted by class walls, Negroes inevitably have special problems in school. Yet it has been clearly demonstrated that, when the walls are scaled or broken down, Negro school achievement levels have improved remarkably.

But whites also suffer from class discrimination, and they too are often denied equal job and educational opportunities. The denial of opportunities to Negroes therefore is only part—a very large part, to be sure—of the problem of class discrimination. The weight of evidence seems to be that *nowhere* in a stratified society are equal opportunities open to all people. In school, as in the world at large, opportunities are usually open to students or closed to them in accordance with their social class position. The higher their position, the more opportunities they have. Or, to put the formula another way: the more students *have*, the more they *get*—in school and in life.

This formula applies to whites as well as to Negroes, and it applies to all social class levels, not just the bottom ones. The social class problems we are dealing with would probably exist even if there were no Negroes in the city —and in fact do exist in all-white school systems. And, if Negroes were given equal opportunities with whites (as of course they must be), the same social class system would continue to exist, though in somewhat modified form. In countries where there is no Negro population at all, social class problems nevertheless exist and are frequently more entrenched than in this country.

So we are dealing with a social class problem, but one which is seriously aggravated and complicated by racial discrimination. In the long run it may turn out that the educational problems of low-income whites are more stubborn and resistant to treatment than those of Negroes. The Negro community is becoming aware of its rights and particularly its rights to equal educational opportunities. Little Rock and the struggle for integration have intensified this interest in education and will probably have a powerful influence on the educational aspirations of Negroes. "Working-class" whites, however, do not have the same urgent educational aspirations and, because they have never been so openly or harshly discriminated against as Negroes, they appear to be less concerned about their rights to equal treatment in the schools.

Social class distinctions therefore will not end when racial discrimination ends. They will end—if at all—only after people at all class levels become completely aware of what these distinctions are, what they mean, and what should be done to end them.

These distinctions go even further than the scope of this

study, since the wealthiest and most privileged groups, who live outside the city limits, were not within the scope of the study. Even within suburban communities there are great distinctions, the highest-income children in suburbia going to private schools, private tutors, exclusive prep and finishing schools in the East, and eventually to Yale, Harvard, Princeton, or elsewhere in the Ivy League. Thus there is a vast separation between the lowest-income groups of Big City and the highest society of suburbia, but only supplementary studies can explore the dimensions of this separation.

In a stratified society, the class structure is shaped rather like a diamond, with the mass layer in the middle, the elite layer at the pinnacle, small groups of social outcasts at the bottom point, and numerous layers in between, each with its own special social class designation and special problems. If we often refer to the contrasts between the lowest and the highest income groups it is only because problems are most obvious at these levels and because it is a short-hand form of referring to social class distinctions. Class problems exist at all layers and are just as serious for middle-income groups (from their own point of view) as for lower-income groups.

Planning the Study

When this project was in the planning stages, it was first decided that perhaps only two schools in Big City would be studied—the highest- and the lowest-income high schools. They had to be high schools, rather than elementary schools, because social class appears to be more visible at the high-school level.

After second thought, the suspicion grew that if only two schools were studied it might turn out that the schools selected were not at all typical of upper- and lower-income schools. Also, if only two schools were studied we would not know how the other schools, the in-between ones, fitted into the social class picture. It seemed desirable therefore to study all the high schools in the city.

This was still not enough. High schools, being larger than elementary schools, draw students from larger geographic areas. Because of this, they tend to have a greater mixture of social classes in their student bodies. We wanted "pure" schools. We wanted to compare upper- and lower-income schools, and so we preferred to study schools in which students came from roughly the same social class background. To find this purity we had to go down to the smaller and more homogeneous elementary schools. Also we found that certain vital information—IQ-test scores, achievement-test scores, etc.—were available for elementary schools but not for high schools.

As we were unwilling to settle for much less than the whole story, it seemed necessary to undertake the rather staggering job of examining all the elementary schools in the city (numbering over two hundred) as well as all the high schools. The high schools had to stay in the study because, as we have said, many important aspects of social class are most obvious at this level. In high school, students are prepared for their future occupations and their future social class positions; some enter the college preparatory curriculum, and others enter vocational or general curriculums. Many drop out of school altogether; these drop-outs would be especially interesting because it was suspected that most of them come from lower-income groups.

To complete the picture, junior high schools in the city were also included. But, since junior highs tend to be located in the lower-income areas of Big City, differences based on income were not so apparent at this level as at the other levels, and, for brevity's sake, data on these schools is not included here.

The city's several trade, vocational, and technical schools were not studied because they are not "neighborhood" schools as the others are, but instead draw students from various income areas of the city. Because of the mixture of students in them, it was impossible to calculate family income by the method of computation used here.

In brief, this is how the study grew to its present size, covering as it does all relevant and available facts about the 285,000 students, 10,000 teachers, and almost 300 schools in Big City.

2

Elementary Schools

Whosoever shall receive this child in my name
receiveth me; and whosoever shall receive me
receiveth him that sent me: for he that is least
among you all, the same shall be great.

—Luke 9:48

ELEMENTARY SCHOOLS

These were the methods used in setting up the study:
First we found out the average family income levels in
each school area. For this purpose, revised census data were
used (the revisions having been made by a local newspaper). It was necessary to use average income figures,
since median income data were not available. Although
average figures are higher than median, they proved to be
just as suitable for our purposes.

Schools with the same or very similar income levels were
then grouped together. These school groups were ranked,
from the lowest to the highest income group. As it turned
out, there were twenty-six groups of schools with separate
and distinct income levels.

Table 1 lists these income groups and also shows the number of schools included in each group.

TABLE 1. Income Groups

MAJOR INCOME GROUP	MINOR INCOME GROUP	AVERAGE FAMILY INCOME, 1957	NUMBER OF ELEMENTARY SCHOOLS IN EACH GROUP
	1	$3500	3
	2	3800	10
Group I	3	4520	5
	4	4700	6
	5	4857	7
	6	5300	9
	7	5500	6
	8	5689	9
	9	5800	13
Group II	10	5900	11
	11	6000	18
	12	6200	2
	13	6312	11
	14	6500	21
	15	6695	7
	16	7100	17
	17	7404	8
	18	7600	17
Group III	19	7700	4
	20	7900	16
	21	8000	5
	22	8207	7
	23	8500	11
	24	9112	16
Group IV	25	9933	1
	26	11,055	3

In addition, this table shows the "major income groups." These major groups are simply divisions which have been made of the minor groups after every $2000 of income.

Thus major group I includes all schools where family income is between $3000 and $5000. (Exception: major group IV includes all schools over $9000, the exception having been made in order to keep this group up to a workable size.)

The table is rather complicated, but it will be necessary to understand it completely in order to move on to other things.

Success or Failure

Achievement Scores

Achievement tests show—perhaps better than any other measure, and certainly better than report-card marks—how much students are learning in school. It may be, of course, that students are learning many important things that do not show up on these achievement tests. And it may also be that these tests include some, perhaps many, detailed bits of information that students do not really need to know. Still, the tests give us a fairly good idea of how well students are coming up to the academic standards which the schools themselves have set.

The test used in Big City is the Iowa Achievement Test, a nationally standardized test which has been given to large numbers of students all over the country. It is claimed to be essentially a test of "skills" rather than simply of facts and information.

The test includes five divisions: language skills, work skills, arithmetic skills, reading, and vocabulary. It will be noticed that three of these five divisions (more than half of the test) have directly to do with verbal skills: reading,

TABLE 2. Iowa Achievement Test Composite Scores

INCOME	INCOME GROUP	FOURTH GRADE	SIXTH GRADE	EIGHTH GRADE
$3000—	1	3.10	5.30	—
	2	3.45	5.06	6.50
	3	3.63	5.32	—
	4	3.55	5.35	7.30
	5	3.46	5.28	—
$5000—	6	3.69	5.50	7.13
	7	3.55	5.40	—
	8	3.58	5.45	—
	9	3.70	5.57	—
	10	3.72	5.61	7.10
	11	3.62	5.54	7.50
	12	3.40	5.50	—
	13	3.80	5.59	—
	14	3.94	5.85	7.70
	15	3.88	5.75	7.44
$7000—	16	4.21	6.16	7.91
	17	4.28	6.38	8.00
	18	4.46	6.45	8.19
	19	4.53	6.60	8.27
	20	4.43	6.49	8.22
	21	4.48	6.68	8.37
	22	4.56	6.62	8.29
	23	4.60	6.80	8.44
$9000—	24	4.78	6.95	8.56
	25	4.90	7.30	9.10
	26	5.10	7.50	9.30

KEY

4.00 = fourth grade
6.00 = sixth grade
8.00 = eighth grade

Note: Blank spaces indicate that there are no students in the elementary schools at the eighth-grade level in these income groups; instead these students are attending junior high schools.

vocabulary, and language skills. The other two sections (work skills and arithmetic skills) also depend on the ability to use language well, since the Iowa tests are written tests and students must be able to read them quickly and accurately in order to do well on them. This is the way it is with most written tests, if not all of them. They lean their whole weight on the student's ability to read and his skill at taking written tests.

In Big City the Iowa test was recently given to all students at three grade levels: fourth, sixth, and eighth; Table 2 shows the relationship between test scores and family income levels.

Three things are immediately striking in this table:

One: All schools *above* $7000 income are achieving *above* grade level (with only one exception in the eighth grade). All schools *below* $7000 income are achieving *below* grade level.

Two: In general, achievement scores tend to go up as income levels go up.

Three: In the fourth grade, group 1 is achieving almost one whole year below grade level. At the same time, group 26 is achieving more than a year above grade level. Thus the highest income group is achieving at a level *two whole years* above the lowest-income group.

The scores in the table are "composite" scores; that is, they are the sum of the scores in the five separate areas: language skills, work skills, arithmetic skills, reading, and vocabulary.

The composite scores for the major income groups show that without exception achievement scores rise with family income levels (Table 3).

TABLE 3. Iowa Composite Scores, Major Income Groups

MAJOR INCOME GROUP	FOURTH GRADE	SIXTH GRADE	EIGHTH GRADE
I ($3000—)	3.48	5.23	6.77
II ($5000—)	3.73	5.61	7.38
III ($7000—)	4.42	6.47	8.22
IV ($9000—)	4.84	7.05	8.67
Difference between groups I and IV	1.36	1.82	1.90

As we see, the difference between groups I and IV becomes greater with each passing grade. In the eighth grade the lowest-income students are almost two years behind the highest-income students. Some observations and explanations that have been made about this situation follow.

Jackson Toby: "School subjects are cumulative. Within a few years, the child from a deprived background is retarded in basic skills, such as reading, absolutely necessary for successful performance in the higher grades. This makes school still more uninteresting, if not unpleasant, and he neglects his work further. Eventually he realizes he can never catch up." [1]

Joseph Kahl: "Social status was not an important factor in the earliest grades; it began to take effect around the fourth grade and had an increasing effect as each year passed." [2]

Howard Becker: "One resultant of this situation—in which less is expected of those teachers whose students are more difficult to teach—is that the problem becomes more aggravated in each grade, as the gap between what the children should know and what they actually do know becomes wider and wider." [3]

Only the composite scores of the Iowa test have been included in these tables. The scores in the five separate areas (language skills, work skills, arithmetic skills, reading, and vocabulary) give us valuable clues about the learning problems of lower-income students. They also tell us something about why upper-income students are so successful in school.

Relatively speaking (relative to their *composite* scores, that is), lower-income groups did well in arithmetic and work skills. Upper-income groups did poorly in these two "non-verbal" areas, relative to their composite scores. Upper-income groups, however, did very well on the reading section of the test, while lower-income groups did worse in reading than in the other areas.

The figures in Table 4 represent the difference between the scores in work skills, arithmetic, and reading in the fourth grade, and the total (or composite) scores. A minus sign before the number indicates that the score was below the composite score, a plus sign that it was above.

TABLE 4. Fourth-Grade Iowa Achievement Scores

MAJOR INCOME GROUP	TOTAL WORK SKILLS *	TOTAL ARITHMETIC *	READING *
I ($3000—)	0	+.09	—.14
II ($5000—)	—.03	+.07	—.06
III ($7000—)	—.09	—.01	+.07
IV ($9000—)	—.19	—.15	+.20

* Relative to total *composite* score.

The greatest difference in these scores is in reading; lower-income groups are unusually weak and upper-income groups are unusually strong in reading. Perhaps this explains why the over-all performance levels of lower-income groups on these tests is below that of upper-income groups.

Approaching these important Iowa scores from still another angle, we see them in perhaps an even more startling perspective.

Table 5 shows the percentage of schools that are above or below grade level in each income group. This table seems to speak for itself—clearly, perhaps eloquently.

TABLE 5. Schools Above and Below Grade Level, Fourth-Grade Composite Iowa Achievement Scores (Percentage of schools in each income group)

	MAJOR INCOME GROUPS			
	GROUP I $3000—	GROUP II $5000—	GROUP III $7000—	GROUP IV $9000—
Schools below grade level	96%	82%	5%	0
Schools a *half*-grade or more below grade level	72	24	0	0
Schools a *full* grade or more below grade level	4	1	0	0
Schools above grade level	4	18	95	100
Schools a *half*-grade or more above grade level	0	1	49	89
Schools a *full* grade or more above grade level	0	0	1	22

Reading

Back to the reading problem. It is true that many educational sins have been committed by champions of the "teach 'em reading and nothing else—and jam it down their throats if you have to" point of view. Yet lower-income groups have serious reading deficiencies that make it almost impossible for them to do well in school.

What is more important, because they cannot read well —with all this implies for other areas of study—they are prevented from moving up into higher-paying occupations, into skilled white-collar business and professional jobs. Their reading and general language disabilities tend to perpetuate their social class position and to keep them in the occupations of their parents. This is far from being the only factor affecting their future class position, but it is an important one.

Perhaps what these lower-income groups need more than anything else is the skill, the knowledge, and enough formal education to enable them to move up into better occupations and into a better life. If they cannot read well, however, it is extremely difficult for them to qualify for skilled jobs and for the higher pay and status these jobs offer.

Success in school seems to be very closely associated with reading skill. Strang has observed, "It is well known that gifted children are great readers." [4] Gray studied dropouts among tenth-graders and found that three times as many poor readers as good readers drop out of school before graduation.[5]

Reading ability is also closely associated with social class. H. A. Coleman studied the performance of junior-high-school students and found that "poor readers, as a group, come with surprising consistency from children of low socio-economic status." [6]

In a study of first-grade children Esther Milner found that all children in the lower-upper and upper-middle classes were high scorers on a reading-readiness test. At the same time, all the children in the lower-lower class were low scorers.[7]

Milner investigated the home environment of children in this study group. She found that the high scorers on this reading test were more likely than the low scorers to own several or a great many storybooks. They were also more likely to have been read to habitually by their parents. As an interesting sidelight, she also found that the low scorers more frequently expressed strong negative feelings about physical punishment administered by their parents; could not recall ever feeling "real happy," or were unable to describe such instances; and said that neither their parents nor any other related adult hugged or kissed or spoke approvingly to them.

What does all this mean? Are these lower-class children poor readers because they are not very bright? Or are they poor readers because their parents do not or cannot read to them, because they have no books at home, because their home environment does not fit them psychologically for reading and for school work? Evidence is that these children *can* learn to read when enough attention is given to them and their reading problems.

One small but impressive piece of evidence that this is true comes from the experience of George E. Bereday of Columbia University. Dr. Bereday invited a Harlem youth from a remedial reading class to visit his office once a week for remedial reading aid. He also invited him to his home one night a week for personal guidance and a chance to practice his reading. The boy, who should have been a fifth-grader, could not read above second-grade level at the time of his first visit. In the first six weeks he improved his reading to fourth-grade level. Bereday said, "There's nothing dumb about this boy. I want eventually to enter him in college. If nothing else, I'll prove that a little compassion, a little time and private attention can save the most hopeless and backward pupil." [8]

The central office of the Board of Education in Big City operates a reading-improvement program in which two types of special classes are offered: after-school and all-day classes. The after-school classes serviced about 720 children in 1957–58; the all-day classes serviced ten schools, into each of which was sent a remedial reading teacher for two full days a week.

This reading-improvement program is new and it appears to be functioning quite well. Perhaps it is not the best possible approach to reading improvement, but in so far as it tries to do *something* about reading problems, it is to be commended. It has certain significant shortcomings, however, which are all too typical of the kind of treatment given in the schools to lower-income students.

In this program, though lower-income students are much more in need of remedial reading attention, more services are given to upper- than to lower-income groups. As we have seen, Iowa Achievement scores indicate that all school groups *below* $7000 are reading below grade level, and that students in these groups seem to have more trouble with reading than with other subjects. On the other hand, all school groups *above* $7000 were above grade level in reading. This obviously indicates that the need for remedial reading classes is far greater in the lower-income groups than in the upper-income groups.

Yet in the after-school reading classes there were more

students from the upper-income half than from the lower-income half. To be exact, for every 10,000 students in each income group there were 23.4 students from the lower-income half (below $7000) and 26.1 students from the upper-income half.

Participation in the all-day reading program was as follows: 3.9 per cent of all schools in the lower-income half and 4.9 per cent of schools in the upper half have an all-day reading teacher. Group III ($7000–$9000) received more services than any other group.

Upper-income groups profited most from this program because it was set up in such a way as to exclude many poor readers from lower-income groups. In order to get into these reading classes it was required that a child have an IQ score of at least C. If he had anything less, he could not qualify for admission. It was reported informally that some children with low IQ scores were admitted to the classes, despite the rule excluding them, but the numbers were unspecified.

The trouble with such exclusive ground rules is that the IQ test, like all written tests, is mainly a test of reading skill. If a child cannot read well he will be very unlikely to do well on IQ tests.

The ground rules, then, work like this: A child is given a reading test (an IQ test). If he does poorly on this reading test he cannot get remedial aid. If he does relatively well on the test, he is eligible for remedial reading aid. A strange logic, but one which is all too often applied in the schools.

Lower-income students are poor readers very often because their parents cannot or do not read to them at home, because they do not have books in their homes, and because, even if they had books, their environment would not be conducive to reading.

They are poor readers because they usually do not use public libraries, have never been taught to use them, have never been properly encouraged by libraries to enter and make themselves at home (in so far as it is possible in these silent, forbidding quarters).

Yet the faulty IQ logic assumes that the child does not learn from books because he is slow or stupid rather than perhaps merely uninformed and uninspired. The application of this logic prevented lower-income children in Big City from getting the kind of help with their reading problems they obviously need.

Remedial reading programs in Big City are not being expanded—to include lower-income groups or anyone else. Budget allocations are not being increased for this purpose. At the same time the extension of "gifted"-child programs servicing upper-income groups is moving forward with accelerated speed.

Lower-income groups have trouble with reading for many reasons. A very significant one we have not yet mentioned has to do with the kind of material lower-income children are required to read in school. Numbers of studies have shown that these materials are based largely on the vocabulary, experiences, and interests of upper-income groups.

William H. Burton, writing in the *Harvard Educational Review*, puts the problem this way: "Books used in beginning reading practically never base content upon the experience known to the whole range of children using the books. The experience of the huge majority is, in fact, usually ignored. The very books designed to teach children to read actually cannot be read by some of the children. Not a single series of readers includes the experience of lower-class children." [9]

This is true not only in beginning reading. The same thing can be said about virtually every text used at every grade level. Seldom do any of these texts speak the language of lower-income students or communicate with them in any meaningful way.

When children are provided with suitable reading materials, adapted to their vocabulary, experiences and interests, surprising results are often produced.

The University of Kentucky once conducted an experimental program based on the assumption that simple, readable, meaningful reading materials would considerably improve the reading skills and also the general standard of living of low-income children. [10]

Specially prepared reading materials dealing with problems of health and diet were introduced into two Kentucky schools. Nothing else in the curriculum was changed; only these special reading materials were added. Guides were also prepared for the teachers, instructing them on the best use of these materials.

The project lasted for ten years. A comparison of students in the two project schools with students in other schools showed that in the experimental group there was a pronounced improvement in fundamental learning skills, especially reading. It also showed that these materials on health and dietary habits had a positive effect on the attitudes of people in these communities and improved their standard of living.

If this can be done in Kentucky, it very likely can be

done elsewhere. Unfortunately little attention has been paid elsewhere to the special reading problems of lower-income groups. In attending to these reading problems, top priority must be given to providing suitable reading materials and texts which students can and will want to read. We would not expect children to learn how to play baseball with a hockey stick and puck. And we should not expect children to learn how to read with books whose language and subject matter are all but incomprehensible to them.

Oscar Handlin, Harvard historian, writes about an earlier but similar generation:

How would the schools help them? By teaching them what was in these books.

Idly the boys fingered the battered volumes from which wisdom was to flow. . . .

This is Jack. This is Jack's house. This is Jack's Daddy. Jack goes shopping. Jack goes to school. On the way he meets a cow. On the way he meets a sheep. Jack comes home. Jack falls asleep. And surely enough, across the top from page to page the brightly colored pictures show it all. Blue-eyed and blond, Jack himself stares out over the nice white collar and the neatly buttoned jacket. Across the green lawn, from the porch of the pretty yellow home, a miraculously slim mother waves. By the side of a road that dips through the fields of corn, the animals wait, each in turn extends its greeting. There it all is, real as life.

Except that it is all a lie. There is no Jack, no house, no brightly smiling "Mummy." In the whole room there is not a boy with such a name, with such an appearance. One can walk streets without end and there will be never a glimpse of the yellow clapboards, of the close-cropped grass. Who sleeps like Jack alone in the prim room by the window to be wakened by singing birds? "Good morning, Mr. Robin." The whole book is false because nothing in it touches on the experience of its readers and no element in their experience creeps into its pages.

Falsity runs through all their books, which all were written to be used by other pupils in other schools: even the arithmetic sets its problems in terms of the rural countryside. Falsity runs through all their education. They learn the songs their mothers never sang. They mouth the precepts with no meaning: "A rolling stone gathers no moss. Make hay while the sun shines." But what stone, what moss, what hay? [11]

Today the agrarian references have usually been removed from the urban texts, but the falsity remains. Jack and Mummy have simply moved into their pretty yellow home in the city.

IQ Scores

The list on page 39 shows the combined IQ scores of children in the first and fourth grades. Several things will be noted in this list.

One: All income groups below $7000 have scores of less than 4.00 (or less than "C" rating). All income groups over $7000 have ratings of better than "C."

Two: Scores tend to go up as income goes up.

Three: The difference between the scores of groups I and IV is only somewhat more than one "letter" grade; that is, group I is somewhat less than C minus, and group IV is only a small fraction above C plus.

INCOME	INCOME GROUP	IQ RATING
$3000—	1	2.57
	2	2.73
	3	2.92
	4	2.86
	5	2.75
$5000—	6	2.79
	7	2.90
	8	3.18
	9	3.08
	10	3.28
	11	3.19
	12	2.95
	13	3.54
	14	3.74
	15	3.59
$7000—	16	4.21
	17	4.27
	18	4.68
	19	4.85
	20	4.56
	21	4.66
	22	4.70
	23	4.86
$9000—	24	5.00
	25	4.95
	26	5.51

KEY

2.00 = D
3.00 = C—
4.00 = C
5.00 = C+
6.00 = B

Scores by major income groups were:

MAJOR INCOME GROUP	IQ SCORE
I ($3000—)	2.79
II ($5000—)	3.31
III ($7000—)	4.55
IV ($9000—)	5.09

Accepted at face value or even with reservations, these IQ scores provide an easy answer to questions raised about the performance levels of lower-income children. Those looking for an easy way out can claim that the blame for low achievement levels lies with the child, and not with the school or the home or society. The child is simply not smart enough to learn much in school, and his IQ score proves it.

But, as we have said before, there is not a shred of proof that any of these IQ tests are valid measures of native intelligence, and in fact there is much proof that they are *not.* Yet, despite the cautions given by the psychologists who devise the tests, they continue to be used in the schools as accurate measures of native ability.

University of Chicago Professor Allison Davis, who has perhaps spent as much time examining the validity of IQ tests as any scholar, says, "There is now clear, scientific evidence that these tests use chiefly problems which are far more frequently met in urban middle-class culture." [12] Because of this he concludes, these tests are not fair to lower-class children.

A five-year study conducted at the University of Chicago, he says, showed that ten of the most widely used standard tests of intelligence are composed of an overwhelming proportion of questions on which the higher occupational groups are superior. This superiority is found, upon study, to be associated with the type of vocabulary used in these standard tests and with the greater training and motivation of the higher occupational groups with regard to these tests.

In recent years scholars have been trying to devise tests

which will be free of this bias against lower-class groups. It apparently is impossible to create "culture-free" tests, however, since cultural bias is so all-pervasive in IQ tests. Much more is involved than simply vocabulary differences or the underdeveloped reading skills of lower-income groups. Motivation is also an important factor. Yale Professor August B. Hollingshead says that the upper-class students in Elmtown high school did better on IQ tests because of greater motivation and because they have a different approach to test-taking: [13]

> Experience imbues them with a need for personal achievement that is expressed in their constant search for success, teaching them from infancy to face each new situation aggressively and to overcome it to the best of their ability. When they take a test, whether it is arithmetic or intelligence, they normally try to do their best on it, for their ego is on trial and they must make good, and they generally do.
>
> On the other hand . . . [the lowest-class] adolescent has been subjected to a family and class culture in which failure, worry and frustration are common. He has not been trained at home to do his best in school. His parents have not ingrained in him the idea that he must make good grades if he is to be a success in life. Moreover, the class system as it functions in the school does not help him to overcome the poor training he has received at home and in the neighborhood.

Sophisticated people—those who devise these tests—are usually well aware of the limitations of their products. But school people rarely are. Even when they are told that the tests do not measure native intelligence, they persist in acting as before, judging and categorizing students according to IQ scores and what is presumed to be their built-in mental capacity.

Because these tests are persistently misused in school, it would seem extremely advisable to abandon their use, and their misuse, completely.

Some of the sophisticated people, however, say that the tests should stay. They are good predictors, it is claimed, of a child's chances for success in school. Of course there are many good predictors of success in school. IQ, it has been discovered, is not as accurate a predictor as other items—teachers' evaluation of students, for example.

Social class is also a fairly accurate predictor of success in school. If you know a child's class status, his family income, his parents' educational levels, you can quite accurately predict what will happen to him in school and how successful he will be.

Yet no one would suggest that children be separated (as they are by IQ score) according to family income, etc., with the best education offered to children from the highest-income families.

In view of the close relationship between social class and IQ scores, the notion that children should be selected and sorted on the basis of IQ scores, simply because these are somewhat predictive of school success, seems just as improper and unreasonable.

Throughout the country great pressure is being put on the schools, with very effective results, to segregate students as soon as they enter school—that is, in the first grade. At this rate, perhaps one day we shall find some system of prenatal segregation being used in the schools. At any rate the pressure for early segregation has built up to such an extent in Big City that the citizens' advisory committee included a recommendation to this effect in its report.

In segregating students the IQ test is used as the principal guide in determining which students are "slow" (and should be made even slower by segregation) and which are "fast" (and should therefore be given special advantages and removed from contamination by other students).

In Big City children are sorted into two main groups on leaving kindergarten: Reading Readiness and First Grade; in other school systems there are more than two divisions. Selections for Reading Readiness are made on the basis of an intelligence test which is supposed to indicate which students are smart enough to enter the first grade and which ones must be held back a semester or two in a Reading Readiness class.

The test used to make this determination is fifteen years old and was written by the director of the Psychological Clinic, among others. In a review of IQ and other tests in his book *Psychological Testing*, James T. Murcell says about the Big City intelligence tests, "Standardization is inadequate . . . the whole interpretation lacks statistical foundation." [14]

This is what the test, which may decide a child's life from the first grade on, is like, and it is rather typical of all the varieties of IQ test. There are twelve pages of test work in it. Four pages of the test are based directly on vocabulary questions. Eight pages contain the following exercises:

1. Matching; match one word or picture with another that is exactly the same.

2. Copying a geometric shape.
3. Copying a drawing which the teacher shows only once and then puts out of sight.
4. Remembering things from a story read earlier in the test by the teacher, and matching with pictures.
5. Remembering a rather long list of words and matching with pictures.

What is perhaps most striking about this and other early elementary IQ tests is that they depend so much on a child's familiarity with rather sketchily drawn pictures. If a child has looked at picture books at home and has had them read to him by adults, he will certainly have a distinct advantage in recognizing pictures in these tests quickly and accurately.

The test of course depends to some considerable extent on how quickly the pictures are recognized. These picture-recognition requirements put lower-income students at a disadvantage, since they are much less likely than upper-income children to have looked at picture books or to have been read to by their parents—since their parents often either cannot read or have so much trouble reading that they would rather not.

In the section of the test that requires children to match one word with an identical one in a list of words (as, match the word "look" with one of the following: book, cook, look, took), the child who has already learned something about word recognition at home again has a distinct advantage. Children in the lowest-income groups seldom have any extra-school experiences with reading, though middle-income children can often recognize many words from having looked at them in picture books or from having been taught to read them.

About one-third of all the pictures in this Reading Readiness test—and it is mostly a picture test—are of animals. Now, most lower-income children are familiar with dogs, cats, mice, and rats (though not necessarily with a sketchy picture), but few know anything about other "domestic" animals, and even fewer know anything about zoo animals. In Big City the zoo is located in an upper-middle-class suburb, far from the heart of the lowest-income areas. One immediately noticeable aspect of zoo attendance is that virtually no Negroes go there, perhaps because it is too far away or inaccessible for other reasons. It may be that few lower-income whites go there, but this is much harder to determine.

Yet on the Big City Reading Readiness IQ test these lower-income children, most of whom have almost no familiarity with animals, are required to recognize pictures of the following animals, among others: chicken, pig, horse, giraffe, monkey, rabbit, hen, elephant, camel, bear, butterfly, squirrel, fish, pheasant. In addition, one whole section of the test is based on a story, read by the teacher, of a family's trip to the zoo and the things they did and the animals they saw there.

As for vocabulary, which comprises about one-third of the test, not counting more indirect vocabulary use, lower-income kindergarten children are required to know the following words, among others, and to recognize pictures of them: candle holder, teapot, vase, book, violin, piano, canoe, sailboat, ocean liner, steeple, flag pole, castle, light house, barn, church (not the store-front variety attended by low-income groups), camera, cash register, typewriter, weighing scale, dwarf. They are also required to choose from the following the "one that sleeps all winter": bear, man, baby, mouse.

Few lower-income children would know that bears sleep all winter, never having seen or perhaps even heard of a bear, and very few would be familiar with the words or objects in the vocabulary section—strange as it may seem to most middle-class adults. It would be an extremely rare child from a low-income neighborhood who would know about and be able to recognize pictures of a castle, a steeple, a light house, a dwarf, a violin, or most of the other objects. These things are not in the range of their experience. They do not have the words in their vocabulary (generally); they seldom know anything about the objects, and even if they did they might not recognize their pictures.

Big City's Advanced First Grade Intelligence test is thirty-five years old and again it was written by the director of the Psychological Clinic.

The test is much like the Reading Readiness test. It mostly involves rapid picture recognition—that is, matching of words with pictures (as the word "sheep" with a picture of sheep). Again, about a third of all the pictures are of animals, many of which are quite unfamiliar to lower-income children. Aside from the speed requirement (which depends on motivation and early training), the test is more a test of vocabulary, picture recognition, and general information than anything else.

The question is asked, for example: which animals have feathers—bird, hen, squirrel, pigeon? Many lower-income children do not know the word "feather." If they did, they might not know whether or not hens and squirrels had them. Moreover they might not be able to recognize pictures of these animals with the required speed, not being practiced in picture-recognition skills.

They are also asked to mark the pictured objects that grow on trees: pumpkin, orange, apple, banana, pear. It would be an extremely rare lower-income child who would be able to make anything at all out of this question.

They are also required to know that a violin (a classically middle-class instrument) is meant to be played on. They are asked which four are alike: baseball bat, tennis racket, heavy shoe, a baseball, a football. A lower-income child would be more likely to think that a heavy shoe was like the others (for use in playing baseball or football, sports with which he is somewhat familiar) rather than a tennis racket, since tennis is generally a middle- and upper-income sport. Yet if he marked the shoe he would be wrong and would get a lower IQ rating as a result.

These are only a few of the items of this sort contained in the test. Like all other IQ tests, it is loaded with culturally biased items, and in fact the whole test is biased in that it depends on early training in picture recognition. It is on the basis of such grossly biased tests that basic, controlling decisions are made about the "native" intellectual ability of students and their present and future place in school life.

Referring to IQ tests used in higher grades, as well as in the early grades, Professors Donald J. Lloyd and Harry R. Warfel discuss the influence of social class and verbal skills on IQ scores: "Persons with high IQs know more words than persons with low IQs, but that is not surprising, because an important part of the test on which the

IQ is based is itself verbal. City people show up with higher quotients on these tests than country people, the children of the well-to-do come off better than the children of the poor, and whites do better than non-whites. An only daughter of well-to-do white city dwellers shows up best of all. Small wonder since the tests are made up by well-to-do white city dwellers and favor their vocabulary. If she were tested on the vocabulary of the poorer non-white country people, she would run a sad race." [15]

Since they seem to be largely a product of training, IQ scores can be changed by outside influences and special preparation.

P. E. Vernon found an average increase of 11 points on IQ scores as a result of a few hours' coaching in material similar to that found in IQ tests.[16] (The difference between the IQ scores of children from professional and managerial families and those from unskilled labor families is in the neighborhood of 15 to 25 points.)

At Whittier College, California, Professor Albert Upton in his course titled "Analytic Thinking" raised his freshmen students' IQ average from 110 to 120 during the course of two semesters. The difference between an IQ of 110 and 120 is the difference between outscoring nine out of ten instead of seven out of ten. In practical terms, it may be the difference between getting into the college of your choice or not going to college at all.

Numerous studies of identical twins and children in institutions, nursery schools and foster homes have shown that IQ scores can be raised by changing the environment, improving reading skills, and teaching children how to take tests. Typical of these studies is the following.

In a study of 19 pairs of identical twins, it was found

that "differences in educational and social environments produce undeniable differences in intelligence and scholastic achievements as measured by our tests." Most of the identical twins had been separated from their first year and brought up in different places.[17]

Other evidence that IQ scores can be changed comes from Cape Canaveral. The children of scientists working at this Florida missile base attend a high school where achievement levels have nearly broken through the ceiling. Odum says about this school:

> What surprises many people and is suggesting new concepts of "intelligence" to educators—an unexpectedly large number of the gifted children belong to families of "ordinary" people—farmers, shopkeepers and others who have no connection with missiles. And the intelligence and achievement levels among all groups of children in Brevard County —mediocre as well as bright students—keep rising.
>
> Why? That is a question for which educators are trying to find an answer. And they suspect that the answer will be important.
>
> Dr. Arthur W. Combs professor of education at the University of Florida says: "For several generations we have been accustomed to thinking of intelligence as a static kind of capacity open to little change or modification. . . . Perceptual psychology now tells us that how a person behaves is a function of his perception . . . Human perceptions are so much within our capacities that we may even be able to create intelligence by helping people to perceive more intensively and more richly, and by creating situations that make it possible for these perceptions to be available when needed."

If Dr. Combs's ideas prove to be correct and can be put to practical application in educational techniques, it could

mean that there is hardly any limit to the intelligence that
can be developed and the learning that can be implanted
in the average human mind.[18]

If IQ tests are so heavily influenced by environmental
factors, why pretend that they measure "native" intelligence, whatever that is? Why not stop using them and substitute achievement tests as a measure of school progress?

It is easy to raise such questions and just as difficult to
answer them. IQ tests are used because they *have* been
used. They are a tradition, and traditions are not easily
tampered with in the schools. They are used because some
teachers and administrators feel—"well, maybe they have
some validity." They are used because many people feel
they need a device for measuring intelligence and separating children into class categories. They are used because
those who oppose their use do not have the courage or
the authority to stop their use.

It is perhaps worth mentioning, in view of recent ad-
miring comments about Soviet education, that IQ tests
are not used in Soviet schools. They are not used, it is said,
because intelligence is not considered an innate quality,
incapable of being changed by environment and instruction; also, it is said that the use of IQ tests tends to retard
the school progress of children who get lower scores.

On the home front, Professor Allison Davis says, "Half
the ability in this country goes down the drain because of
the failure of intelligence tests to measure the real mental
ability of the children from the lower socio-economic
groups, and because of the failure of the schools to recognize and train this ability." [19]

IQ tests retard the progress of lower-income children

(and perhaps of all children who get anything less than top ratings) because they tend to put students in pigeonholes, where they sit complacently throughout most of their school lives.

IQ categories in fact can be more rigid than social class. It is more realistic for a poor child to long for riches than for a low-IQ child to long for a high IQ—if we assume that the IQ is a natural gift and not an acquisition.

In view of the close relationship between IQ scores and social class in Big City, it seems that one very destructive function of the IQ score is that it serves as a kind of cement which fixes students into the social classes of their birth. IQ is the supreme and unchallengeable justification for the social class system. In this sense it is rather like the "divine right of kings," which provided an unchallengeable justification for the system of royal authority. Just as the right to rule was given to kings by God, so is the right to rule given to upper classes by "nature" and by virtue of what they presume to be their superior IQs.

People at all levels often come to accept their IQ rating as they would never accept their social class status. This acceptance tends to retard the growth of students in school, and especially the growth of lower-income students who often get low scores on IQ tests. Typically, the lower-income child comes to school and sooner or later he learns that he cannot compete with upper-income students. He has too many cultural disadvantages. Usually he does not have as much "book knowledge" or as much experience with the world outside his own neighborhood; his language is poor, he cannot read very well, he is often troubled emotionally, he does not have as much will to succeed or as much confidence that he *can* succeed.

For these reasons he does poorly on IQ tests. The teacher learns that he has a low IQ rating and puts him into a slow-moving group where he is not expected to do much or given much attention. He is bright enough however to catch on very quickly to the fact that he is not considered very bright. He comes to accept this very unflattering appraisal because, after all, the school should know. Now he is in his pigeonhole. He can't get out and, what is more, he doesn't try; he accepts his fate. His parents also accept it, since, after all, the schools should know. Intellectually he is lost. He has accepted this low appraisal of himself, and both he and society must suffer the consequences.

The problem of defining intelligence, the limitations of intelligence tests, and the psychological impact of the tests on the low scorer have been summed up editorially by the *New Republic:*

> Any test of over-all intelligence would have to evaluate a man's ability to solve all kinds of problems within the range of human experience. Although an IQ test makes no such claim, laymen who employ test scores often assume it does, disregarding warnings that the ability to solve short abstract problems under pressure is but one facet of "intelligence."
>
> The most obvious limitation on an IQ test is that it measures only ability to solve symbolic problems posed in words, numbers, or pictures. But many other problems derive directly from human experience and require no symbolic analysis. . . . It hardly makes sense to call a man "intelligent" if he cannot solve moral or social problems. . . .
>
> Essentially an IQ test does not pose intellectual problems but mental puzzles. The important talents of a man who

wants to crack the IQ barrier are speed and accuracy, not memory or perspective. . . .

A related difficulty is that if you take an IQ test you are asked only to analyze certain set problems and come up with one "right" answer. You are never asked to synthesize rather than analyze, or to imagine a variety of possibilities rather than to determine one actuality. . . . Researchers at the University of Chicago . . . found that the most "creative" students . . . often had unimpressive IQs, while many whom an IQ test would classify as "genius" turned in stolidly unimaginative performances. And similarly when researchers take a look at the IQs of highly creative scientists they find that many of these men do worse on IQ tests than their less productive colleagues.

Taken together these limitations mean that a man can be socially imperceptive, personally insensitive, and morally obtuse, as well as scatterbrained, shortsighted, and unimaginative, all while being classified as supremely intelligent on the IQ meter. Under such circumstances anyone who relied on an IQ test to discover intellectual potential would be about as silly as a football coach looking for athletic potential who relied on how many pushups every candidate can do.

Yet so long as men have faith in IQ tests, they are bound to "work." . . . If a student coming from kindergarten with a low IQ is automatically pushed into a "slow" first grade section (unless his influential parents make a fuss), he will quickly realize that other people think him dull, and will in most cases accept the label and become so.[20]

Failures

From what has been seen of achievement scores it could be expected that lower-income students would "fail" more often in school than upper-income students. And they do. In the lowest-income group (group 1, $3500), 10.9 per cent of all students in Big City failed to be promoted to a higher grade in January 1958. This means that more than one out of every ten students in this group were not passed at the end of the school year.

What about the other end of the scale? In group 26 (the highest-income group, $11,055), less than 1 per cent (.8 per cent) of all students failed to be promoted. The failure rate in the lowest-income group therefore was more than ten times greater than the rate in the highest-income group.

The following were the non-promotion percentages for the major income groups.

INCOME GROUP	NON-PROMOTION PERCENTAGE
I ($3000—)	7.4%
II ($5000—)	4.9
III ($7000—)	2.9
IV ($9000—)	1.2

By income halves (below and above $7000 income) the rates were as follows.

A (below $7000)	5.5%
B (above $7000)	2.6

Is there anything wrong with this picture? Should there have been more or fewer failures, or is this just about right? It is hard to say. Sometimes failing students does them some good. Sometimes it scares them (and more often their parents) into producing enough at least to get by. Usually it does not. In general, failure does not inspire students with the kind of confidence, trust, and ambition that are required for success in school. It is unfortunate, in a sense, that it does not. Failure—if it produced results —would provide an easy answer to a great many school problems, and some students seem to be so richly deserving of it that it is hard to refrain from failing them simply for vengeance's sake.

But the fact is that failure does not seem to arouse in students the desire to reform and to knuckle down to school tasks. On the contrary, just as "nothing succeeds like success," nothing seems to be more discouraging than repeated failure. Not only is it discouraging, but like other forms of punishment it often tends to intensify the hostil- ities of students toward school, society, their parents, and themselves. In this sense, failure in school may add its own substantial contribution to the high rates of delin- quency and emotional disturbance among the lower- income groups who are frequently failures in school.

Big City schools seem to be at least somewhat accepting of the idea that high failure rates are not generally desir- able, judging by failure rates as compared with achieve- ment levels. Of course failure rates are rather high in some income groups. The rate in group I is more than six times higher than the rate in group IV. Still, the failure rate in group I is very low compared with what it might be. As we have seen, 96 per cent of all schools in group I were below grade level on the Iowa Achievement Tests. Yet only 7.4 per cent of students in group I failed to be pro- moted. Obviously a great many students in this group who are achieving far below grade level are being promoted to higher grades. They are not being failed. Neither are they learning very much in school, judging by achievement tests. Automatic promotion, then, also leaves much to be desired.

But where do we go from here? If failure does not help much, what can be done when a student lags far behind grade level? Ideally, of course, we give the student extra help, enough to raise his achievement levels to where they should be. We talk with him about his problems; we talk to his parents; we see that all his basic health and psychological needs are attended to; we give him extra help with his school work; we give him some incentive to learn.

But what if teachers do not have time for this? A teacher may have a class of forty students, or she may even have six classes of forty students each, all of whom are doing failing work. Can she give them all enough extra help to raise them up to grade level?

What if there are no counselors in the school (and there are none in Big City elementary schools)? What if there are no psychological testing or treatment services, no way to get glasses for the child who can't read without them, or dental care for the child whose teeth are rotting, or an adequate diet for the child who is undernourished, or shoes for the child who can't come to school because he doesn't have them? What do we do then? If the child, under present school conditions, cannot get the attention he needs to raise him to grade level, should we promote him anyway and hope that somehow things will come out all right?

Perhaps we should. If there are only two choices, failure or promotion, perhaps we should choose the lesser of the two evils, promotion. At least if the child is promoted he will have *some* chance, though the unfortunate truth seems to be that he won't have *much* chance. A child who is promoted despite serious academic deficiences is saved the discouraging and often bitter experience of failure, but he doesn't learn much either. He goes into higher grades, nobody paying much attention to him, and finds that he can't do the work at these higher levels. He finds that he is operating academically at, say, a fourth-grade level when others are operating at a fifth-grade level. So he can't learn. The next year is even worse. Since he didn't learn anything last year, he finds that others are now operating at the sixth-grade level, while he is still at the fourth-grade level. It becomes increasingly difficult for him to catch up or to learn anything. Even though he has not "failed," he knows that he is a failure.

But what if he goes to a school where all the other students are in the same boat and none of them are learning very much? In such a situation it may take the student some time to find out that his learning achievements leave much to be desired. He has only the others in his class to compare himself with, and they are all in the same situation. But sooner or later—when he enters high school, when he applies for a job, or perhaps when he decides to go to college—he will discover, and probably in a rather shocking way, that he can't keep up, that he hasn't learned enough, or acquired the academic skills and interests necessary to pull him through. The day of awareness is delayed, but eventually it comes.

Automatic promotion is an easy way out for the schools, but it is not necessarily an easy way out for students. Where promotion is automatic, nobody gets very excited or disturbed about educational problems, and school affairs run along quite smoothly. But the present situation in our schools seems to call for a great deal of excitement and disturbance. One very good way to get it would be to fail all students who "should" be failed because they are achieving below grade level. It would mean in the lower-income schools that virtually the whole student body would be failed. Perhaps then so much excitement would be created—on the part of students, parents, administrators, the public—that the situation might possibly attract the constructive attention it so desperately needs. The situation, of course, would become a public scandal—but it already *is* a public scandal, only nobody knows about it.

Facing facts, however, and human nature, no principal or administrator is going to allow most of the students in his school to be failed, and few people would advocate such a drastic step, if for no other reason than that it has never been done before and the feeling is strong in educational circles that nothing should ever be done for the first time. Furthermore such mass failures would be regarded by school administrators as a reflection on them and a source of trouble and embarrassment. At any rate, though it would make an extremely interesting experimental project, mass failure is perhaps not a practical or desirable solution to the problem of mass under-achievement.

So, since neither failure nor automatic promotion provides the kind of solution we are looking for, we must of necessity return to our original solution: extra attention and lots of it to the learning problems of low-achieving students. No other solution will work.

The "Gifted"-Child Program

Shortly after Sputnik and the sudden alarm about Soviet scientific development, Big City set up a special city-wide program for "gifted" children. Since Soviet schools do not segregate the "gifted" (except the artistically "gifted"), it is strange that concern about Soviet education should have finally put such a program into operation.

The fact is that a heated and protracted debate in the Soviet during the last few years ended in complete defeat for the scientists who proposed the segregation of the scientifically "gifted."

But perhaps Sputnik was simply an excuse for doing what some influential people in the schools wanted to do anyway.

The program was set up for the first year of high school (ninth grade) and 436 students were selected from among all eighth-grade students in the city. The selected students were then sent to special schools to take part in an intensified program of study, with the best possible facilities and teachers available for their instruction. One of the schools offering this program was a technical school; the other two were among the highest-income high schools in the city.

Selections were made on the basis of IQ and Iowa Achievement Test scores. All students had to have at least an A IQ rating, and all had to be achieving at least at grade level.

Table 6 shows the income groups from which these "gifted" children came. The pattern of selection is quite astonishing. Not one of the 436 students selected came from an income group below $5000! At the same time, 148 students came from the highest-income group, even though there were almost 10,000 fewer students in this group than in the below-$5000 group.

In this table, in order to provide a more complete pic-

ture of selections, major income group divisions have been
made after every one thousand dollars of income rather
than after every two thousand.

TABLE 6. Program for "Gifted" Children

INCOME GROUP	NUMBER OF "GIFTED" CHOSEN	RATE PER 10,000 STUDENTS
I (below $5000)	0	0
II ($5000—)	4	1.1
III ($6000—)	41	6.1
IV ($7000—)	120	20.1
V ($8000—)	123	36.0
VI (over $9000)	148	78.8

By income halves, the rate per 10,000 students was:

A (under $7000)	3.7
B (over $7000)	34.4

It appears that this "gifted"-child program is servicing
upper-income groups almost exclusively. Perhaps this explains why so many spokesmen for upper-income groups
have fastened upon "gifted"-child programs as a major
solution to our educational problems. "Educate the elite,"
they say, "and forget about the others." The "elite," of
course, often includes themselves and their own children.

Big City has recently started a second program for the
"gifted." This is an extremely costly program because it
involves after-school and Saturday classes. Although the
eventual scope of this program is still not known, the
present plan is to set up about one hundred classes in a
variety of subjects for elementary and high-school students
in the fifth through twelfth grades.

Roughly estimated, the cost of this program as presently

proposed will be about $40,000 for twenty weeks, not counting the substantial administrative costs involved in organizing and maintaining the program. Since students will be selected on roughly the same basis as in the first program, it can be assumed that upper-income groups will be the main beneficiaries of these costly services. Of course all services for the "gifted" tend to be costly. Recommendations to the citizens' committee in Big City suggests that all special classes for the "gifted" be limited to a class size of no more than twenty-five students. It is also suggested that extra staff and facilities be provided for these classes.

Are upper-income children really so much more "gifted" than lower-income children? If lower-income groups were afforded the same educational advantages as upper-income groups would their children be just as "gifted"? They might be, and there is evidence that they would be.

E. N. Drews, for example, claims that today "there is more intellectual stimulation in the average home," and consequently more and more "gifted" children are coming from homes in the middle and lower-middle economic strata.[21] Other things contributing to this upsurge of intelligence among lower economic groups, she says, are "better schools, better teachers, a widening contribution to intellectual opportunity afforded by television, radio, movies, books, magazines and newspapers."

These chosen ones, then, receive their "gifts" not from nature but from exposure to TV, radio, better schools, etc. Presumably if these and other "social gifts" were more equitably distributed, most normal children might then be considered "gifted." If we wish to do something about the gifted, therefore, we might be much better off distributing more gifts to more children rather than heaping them on a few children who already have received more than their share and who will get along very well no matter what the schools do for them.

This is not to say that there is no justification for offering special classes to advanced students. It is only to say that wholesale segregation of this sort produces doubtful moral and intellectual results in both the "gifted" and the others. In addition, since it is a source of class distinction, it is contrary to the ideals of our free society.

It has never been demonstrated that the segregated "gifted" learn any more than the unsegregated "gifted." The evidence is that they do not.

Dr. Arnold Meier, in charge of curriculum studies for Detroit schools, says that a three-year study of four hundred students in two junior high schools had failed to reveal any significant difference between students in ability groups and those in mixed classes.

Paul Witty in his book *The Gifted Child* concludes: "Sufficient data are not available to warrant an unqualified endorsement of segregation, since the practice is of fairly recent origin and experimental data are inconclusive. . . . The results of studies of segregation are not consistent." [22]

Others have contended, with only eyewitness evidence, that segregation often injures the "gifted" child by making him a follower, a second-rater among his "gifted" peers, whereas in the mixed class he is often a leader and the first in his group.

It would seem obvious that when the "gifted" are separated from the less privileged student they are denied the contacts and leadership responsibilities that can, when properly guided, give them a kind of moral depth not provided in books or in simple academic pursuits.

At the same time they are often thrown into intense and rather unproductive competition with other "gifted" ones. In this overcharged setting tensions often build feverishly, and the burden of study and competition can become an exhausting and demoralizing strain. Good as the school's intentions may be, the ending can be an unhappy one for the "gifted," as suggested in John Hersey's *The Child Buyer*.[23]

What is more, the effect on the "other" child can also be tragic. As many teachers and most people with intimate knowledge of the "other" child know, being assigned an inferior status in school can result in bitter resentment, rejection of school and learning, and an enduring hostility toward the chosen ones (the "eggheads"). Even worse, it can result in acceptance of inferior status.

In the larger society it can result in *The Rise of the Meritocracy*[24] and in a style of life as repelling as the one predicted in *1984*.

Who Is the "Gifted" Child? It is commonly agreed that the "gifted" child is one with a Stanford-Binet IQ score of 140 or over. Almost all schools select students for special programs on the basis of IQ scores—often plus achievement-test scores.

Yet in a moment of insight and frankness the Harvard University admissions committee reports: "We are aware that high test scores and top class ranking in secondary school are not . . . very reliable evidence of real quality, intellectual or otherwise. . . . We are concerned lest we overvalue the conformist boy of high verbal facility who has always kept his nose clean, done what was expected of him and gone blinkered down the middle of the road grinding out top grades as he went. . . . Passion, fire, warmth, goodness, feeling, color, humanity, eccentric individuality—we value these and do not want to see them give way to meek competence." [25]

The bookish child, it appears, rather than the creative child, has the better chance of being labeled "gifted." Horace Mann Bond's study of Merit Scholarship winners revealed that among professional groups, and, in fact, among *all* occupations, the librarian's child was the most likely to win a Merit Scholarship. His chances of winning this coveted award were even greater than those of the offspring of college professors, college presidents, doctors, lawyers, and judges.[26]

Studies show that the "gifted" are often heavier than they are strong, that they are superior in health but inclined toward sedentary pursuits, and that they tend to turn to solitary intellectual play or to reading.

They show that the "gifted" often "have a lack of respect for persons who are less bright than they are, and a tendency to show off in situations where they have information and thinking ability beyond the level of the average person." [27]

As for school achievement, often used as a basis for selecting the "gifted," T. B. Edwards of the University of California (Berkeley) studied 3750 high-school students from 13 high schools in the San Francisco Bay area, with the following conclusions: girls receive better grades than boys; girls are more likely than boys to be prudent; strongly prudent students receive more A and B grades than strongly theoretic students.[28]

Other researchers suggest that "the final test of talent is in the *productiveness of the individual,* that talent is more than intellect," that it is a function of the total personality. Talent, then, they define as "the emergence in *action* of a product growing out of the unique qualities of the individual in their interaction with his external environment —the men, materials, and circumstances of his life" (my italics).[28]

This is seldom the definition used in selecting the "gifted." If it were, selection would be impossible, for talent then becomes something so intangible as to be incapable of assessment or prediction by the measuring machines.

Another research team found, in a study of the total school population of a Midwestern city, that among students in grades two to five with scores on the Stanford-Binet IQ test of 150 or over, almost half (49 per cent) were the offspring of college professors, and a total of 73 per cent were from either business or professional families. Not one child was from an unskilled family.[29]

In the same study it was found that 77 per cent of the mothers of these "gifted" ones had been to college, and 91 per cent had high-school diplomas. A psychological test (Rorschach) was given these students and the results showed that this group had little emotional disturbance, good ego control, and *unexpectedly poor creativity*. Only 26 per cent were rated as spontaneously developing new ideas, and 31 per cent were rated as "not having creative work as a strong point."

The researchers conclude with this question: "Is it possible that Terman in *Genetic Studies of Genius,* in describing the multiple superiority of the gifted child, is simply describing children from the upper socio-economic levels? If this is so, many of our assumptions about the 'differences' of the gifted which call for special educational approaches and methods will need to be reconsidered."

Not only class, but also ethnic group can affect "gifted" ratings. Students coming from ethnic cultures that put high values on learning are apparently more likely to score high on the tests of giftedness.

A study made by Sam Welles and reported in *Fortune,* for example, found that 70 per cent of all students in New York City's schools for the "gifted" (High School of Music and Arts, Bronx High School of Science, Stuyvesant High School for math and science, etc.) were Jewish; yet the Jewish population of New York City is only 27 per cent of the total.[30]

Herline Slocomb, in examining a Seattle high school, asserts that the "gifted" are not neglected, that claims of their neglect are pure myth. According to the records of this school, the "gifted" were all getting a "heavy load of academic subjects" and were the mainstay of extracurricular activities.[31]

Certainly the "gifted" are not neglected by the researchers and the foundations. Even the federal government, a rich patron of research, has been putting its money on the "gifted." One federal agency alone, the Office of Education, Cooperative Research Program, is supporting twenty-seven special projects for children with special abilities, to which it is contributing about $1.5 million.

This sum, contributed by *one* agency for *research* purposes alone, is compared with the sum of $1 million in foundation money being invested in the special *education* of all culturally deprived children in seven major cities. Aside from funds being spent in New York City, this appears to be the only significant sum of money being spent on the education of the underprivileged. So far as this author is aware, *no* significant funds have been given to *research* about the culturally deprived, the underprivileged, the children of unskilled workers.

Nor are the "gifted" neglected in the national education budget. Each year about $3.6 billion is spent in this country on higher education at the college level for the "gifted" child. This amounts to about one dollar for every four spent on public-school education for *all the nation's children.*

In almost all "gifted"-child programs, selections are made on the basis of IQ scores. As we have seen, IQ tests have absolutely no proven validity as tests of native ability. They depend on the child's motivation, his interest in taking tests, his ambition and competitive drive. Nor are the tests "reliable." IQ scores vary from year to year and even from hour to hour, depending on how the child feels at the moment, whether he has had enough to eat or enough sleep, his physical and emotional health, the weather, the time of day, etc. They also appear to change, for better or worse, depending on the child's social class background.

The IQ scores of lower-income students seem actually to decline with the passing school years, as the burden of their inferior social status increases. Some indications of this decline were apparent in the selections made for the "gifted"-child program in Big City.

After the students had been chosen for this program it was discovered that a number of them had been selected by mistake on the basis of their fourth-grade, rather than eighth-grade, IQ scores. The fourth-grade scores had been used because these students had not yet taken the eighth-grade test. When the mistake was discovered, these students were given the eighth-grade IQ test. When the new scores were checked, it was found that the IQ ratings of seventy-two of these students (the total number who took the test at this point was unknown) had changed between the fourth and the eighth grades.

In the case of forty-five of these seventy-two students, the IQ scores had declined so much that they had to be dropped from the "gifted"-child program. A substantial number of these students were from lower-income schools. In one lower-income junior high school ($5000 income) the scores of ten students had declined so much that they were dropped from the "gifted" program. As a result there were no students admitted from this school.

Two other students from low-income junior high schools (below $5000) were also dropped because their IQ scores had declined below the eligibility level. In the case of one of these students the IQ score had changed from A** (the highest rating) in the fourth grade, to C+ in the eighth grade.

It is extremely interesting, considering the rather unquestioning respect paid IQ ratings in the city's schools, that no records are kept in Big City of these changing IQ scores. No comparison has ever been made by the Psychological Clinic, which administers the tests, or by anyone else, of student IQ scores at various grade levels. In fact it was impossible to get anything but composite scores from the first and fourth grades. The separate scores are not even known—by *anyone* in the schools! Yet the whole justification for these tests of "native intelligence" rests on what some testers claim to be the essential constancy and unchanging character of human intelligence. If scores in the fourth grade are substantially different from those in the first grade, then these tests obviously have no validity as tests of "native, inborn, unchanging intellectual ability."

The evidence from "gifted"-child selections seems to indicate that IQ scores change over a very broad range and are much influenced by environmental privilege or deprivation, the scores of many lower-income students actually declining with the passing school years. A comparison of separate scores in the first and fourth grades might well show that the IQ scores of lower- and upper-income students are more nearly equal in the first grade— before environment has had its full effect—than in the fourth grade. In view of all the rather trivial data compiled on Big City schools, it seems quite unexplainable that such comparisons have never been made.

Delinquency

Now that we are acquainted with the children who do well in school—the "gifted"—let us turn to the others, the failures, the problem children, the delinquents.

These are the children, as University of Chicago Professor Robert J. Havighurst has put it, whose "fathers are seldom or never at home and pay little attention to them when they are." These are the children who "come to school in the morning unwashed and in dirty clothes, sometimes without breakfast, often needing a doctor's care. They have trouble learning to read, the first thing in a long series of school difficulties. Their second disadvantage is verbal intelligence below average—a serious handicap in a society that places more and more reliance on verbal agility. Finally, the school fails this group. When they are very young the teacher too often passes over their problems. She is so busy with those who get along passably well that she may allow these three or four children in her class to drift. Eventually, at thirteen or fourteen, they are reading at the level of third or fourth graders but are in the seventh or eighth grade. At about this point they become troublesome problems to the school and grow more so in the ninth grade or the freshman year of high school." [32]

When such students become troublesome in Big City schools they may be put in an "Ungraded Class" or they may be sent to a special school for problem children. If they commit a crime they may end up in the Detention School, which is operated by Big City's board of education. Information was available only on enrollments in Ungraded Classes and the Detention School; the social class origins of students in the several special schools for problem children (sometimes euphemistically called trade or vocational schools) were not known.

The Ungraded Class: This special class is called "Ungraded" because it is made up of students from different grade levels, much like a one-room school. These classes are held in regular schools and children are put into them when they are too troublesome for regular classes.

The "Ungraded Class" is not for the retarded student but rather for the child who is considered a behavior problem. The retarded, the handicapped, and the sickly are often put in other special classes, which are also ungraded. The rate per 10,000 students in each income group in these "Ungraded Classes" was as follows.

INCOME GROUP	STUDENTS IN UNGRADED CLASSES
I ($3000—)	37.7
II ($5000—)	14.8
III ($7000—)	4.2
IV ($9000—)	0

Detention School: The same pattern of distribution holds for admissions to the city's Detention School. This school is operated by the board of education and is attached physically to the juvenile court. Its function is to educate school-age youths who are serving brief sentences in the Detention Home, or who are being held pending trial or transfer to another institution.

Some of the students in this school (one out of eleven) are simply homeless youths who have committed no crime but are being held in the Detention Home (often with serious juvenile offenders) because there is *no other place in the city for them to live*—a brutal indication of the neglect of children who are in trouble and without means.

In analyzing admissions to the Detention School two types of divisions have been used: admissions from regular elementary schools, and admissions from regular schools *plus* admissions from the city's special schools for problem children.

The distribution of youths in the Detention School who were previously enrolled in a *regular* Big City school was (per 10,000 students in the schools of origin) as follows.

INCOME GROUP	DETENTION SCHOOL STUDENTS FROM REGULAR SCHOOLS
I ($3000—)	31.3
II ($5000—)	21.7
III ($7000—)	6.9
IV ($9000—)	2.7

The enrollment in Detention School is topheavy with students from lower-income groups. But, when those students are included who were admitted to the school from the special schools for problem children, the distribution is even more unbalanced, as the following figures indicate.

INCOME GROUP	DETENTION SCHOOL STUDENTS
I ($3000—)	85.7
II ($5000—)	40.2
III ($7000—)	6.9
IV ($9000—)	2.7

The rate of admissions in group I is *thirty-two times greater* than the rate in group IV. Quite the reverse of admission rates to the "gifted"-child program! While the "gifted" come almost exclusively from upper-income groups, the delinquents apparently come almost exclusively from lower-income groups.

Why is delinquency so much more common among lower-income youths? In our present state of at least semicivilized awareness, few people would claim that delinquents are "born that way." Delinquents are made, not born; that much is known.

But if the youths themselves and their "perverse natures" are not to blame, who or what *is?* Parents, neighborhood environment, schools, society? Perhaps all share in the blame, some more than others. But this study is concerned mainly with the schools and with the role they play in the training of youth, so we shall restrict ourselves to a brief consideration of school policies which may contribute to delinquency.

Item: The schools give better services and more of them to upper-income groups. Lower-income groups and their problems are generally neglected.

Item: The school "culture," being predominantly middle class, tends to alienate the lower-income child. Since he cannot share the values of the school, he is inclined to rebel against them in order to assert his own values.

Item: Because schools are often dominated by "female" attitudes, interests, and standards of behavior, lower-income boys (who seem to place a much higher value on masculinity than do upper-income boys) have difficulty finding a place in school life. Lower-income boys, judging by Detention School admissions, are heavily overrepresented in the delinquency statistics.

Item: The schools do not spend any real money on treatment for emotionally disturbed delinquents. Nor do they spend more than token sums on counseling services for lower-income, delinquency-prone youths. Nor do they make much effort to reach the parents of lower-income youths to help them or to consult with them about the behavior and welfare of their children. Upper-income parents, when their children are in trouble, can afford to pay for private care.

Item: Too many people in the schools are convinced

(though usually only in private) that lower-income "troublesome" children are not worth very much and that the
"gifted" students are the only ones that really matter. Too
few people are concerned in any significant way about
lower-income, delinquency-disposed youths, and too little
time, attention, and money is being spent on the solution
of their problems.

The pre-delinquent child is not completely neglected
in Big City. A delinquency-prevention program is now
operating in five Big City schools. It will soon be expanded to twelve schools. The ultimate goal is to include
all schools in the city, in low- as well as high-delinquency
areas.

This program (School-Community Behavior Project)
is a simple one. Its main function is to set up school action
teams composed of these members: two or more classroom
teachers, visiting teacher, attendance officer, school nurse,
and various agency consultants.

The team meets periodically in school, examines the
records of students referred by classroom teachers for anti-
social behavior, and then refers them for treatment to
community agencies. This is done in consultation with
community agencies that may have contact with the child
or may be able to help him.

The program has been in operation since 1953. During
that period a total of 253 children have been involved.
Children with police records are not referred, only those
who *may* become delinquent.

The funds for the program have been supplied by a local
agency. The only financial contribution made by the board

of education is in the form of payment to substitute teachers who fill in when classroom teachers attend action team meetings.

It is not known how effective this program has been. Nor can it be known what might have happened to the students had they not been processed through the program. They might have been more anti-social; on the other hand, they might have been less anti-social. There is no sure way of knowing. The reasonable assumption is, however, that the program is a valuable one.

Arthur C. Johnson, Jr., who has worked with delinquent youths, claims that the rewards-and-punishment system of the school actually fosters delinquency and criminality in some children. He says: "Hark back to our own school days for a picture of the boy who must be 'sat on.' There was John in our class. For any of many reasons, this boy was made to feel alien—a misfit in the group. He got less consideration than we. Sooner or later, he accepted our attitude as a challenge and reacted accordingly. Reaction followed one of two characteristic patterns: either the boy started an indiscriminate bedevilment of teacher and pupils alike; or abandoning the social approach, he became moody and sullen, subject to violent outbursts of temper on the slightest provocation." [33]

Johnson quotes these very colorful and revealing statements of boys who ended up in court:

The teacher tried to make me wear better clothes like the other children. I finally told her to go to hell and walked out. I swore then that I would have better clothes if I had to steal them and I did.

My mother was going nuts and I was worried about her. One day the teacher called me crazy too. I never went to school regular after that.

I was fired from school because I wouldn't study my history. When they brought me back and tried to make me study history again, I started to skip school.

I just couldn't recite in class. The teacher nagged at me and to avoid trouble, I left school.

One day I got to school late and was told that if I couldn't get there on time, not to come at all. I took them at their word.

Albert Cohen, a sociologist at Indiana University, says: "If by the rules of the game, you are no account, one thing you can do is get together with other losers and change the rules. Good becomes bad and bad, good. Toughness, indifference toward school becomes the new norm. You may even acquire stature in the group by defiance of authority and by being punished. Middle-class families equip a child before he gets to school with much of the behavior and skills that the school is called upon to inculcate. Teachers, faced with the problem of keeping order in the classroom, like children who show ambition, achievement, are willing to stick to a job, speak correct English, and are neat and able to control their emotions. This is not because the teachers are undemocratic, but their democracy takes the form of judging all by the same standards, and these are the standards of the middle-class home." [34]

Martin B. Loeb, writing in the *Harvard Educational Review*, says that one of the major characteristics of this middle-class culture, which provides the single standard of behavior in the schools, "is the emphasis on propriety.

In other words, more official rules are found in the middle class than are found in other places—more overtly stated guides of behavior." [35]

Not only are there more rules, but the rules are often very different from those governing lower-status culture. Loeb probes deeper into the psychological characteristics and the values of this dominant culture. "It may be described in psychoanalytic terms," he says, "as the most anal culture. By this, we mean there is an emphasis on ownership of goods, especially home and land, that it is a home-centered culture, that there is emphasis on cleanliness and tidiness, that there is an avoidance of all forms of overt aggression, and that there is an avoidance of expressions of emotions generally, except on highly ritualized occasions such as birth and death. This organizational life provides many stated and formal rules for behavior. However, in general, core cultural guides are not readily stated but appear in terms of what one ought or ought not to do or what 'nice people do.' "

Thus middle-class culture is controlled, clean, tidy, non-violent, unemotional, "nice," home-centered, and very concerned about material possessions.

We make no judgments about this culture. Perhaps, with some important modifications, this is the culture that *should* dominate our schools. This point will not be debated. It should be emphasized, however, that middle-class culture, whatever its virtues or faults, is very different from lower-class culture and, because it *is,* the lower-class child often has great difficulty adjusting in school. When he can't or won't make the adjustment, he becomes disturbed and often rebellious. The school rejects *him,* and so he will reject the *school* and along with

it most other symbols of adult authority. In this way the
school, unwittingly to be sure, becomes a primary cause
of his delinquent behavior.

William H. Burton explores this theme further in the
Harvard Educational Review, confirming and adding
other dimensions to these observations about the middle-
class culture of the school:

> Many teachers simply cannot communicate with lower-
> class children and have no idea of the beliefs and motives of
> these children. The children in turn trying to communicate
> are abashed at criticism of their language and behavior
> which is quite acceptable within their own social group.
>
> The school has generally been geared to the aims, ambi-
> tions, moral or ethical standards of the white, prosperous,
> middle-class, Protestant, Anglo-Saxon population.
>
> Many lower-class children simply do not value the objec-
> tives and the processes of the school, hence do not try. The
> school immediately dubs these children "unintelligent," "un-
> cooperative" or "stubborn." The old class clichés may enter;
> the children are lazy, shiftless, irresponsible. The facts are
> that the school often simply does not meet their needs or
> ambitions, does not operate within their framework of values
> and motivations.
>
> The middle-class regime simply does not socialize the
> lower class children. They are neither believers nor partici-
> pants in the cultural heritage of middle-class society.[36]

If the schools cannot tolerate certain aspects of lower-
class behavior, as these informed observations indicate,
perhaps they can at least work out better ways of changing this behavior. Preaching and simple force (physical
or otherwise), which are the principal means of persuasion

now in use, have not been notably successful in changing behavior. Perhaps the schools should devise more persuasive systems of rewards and punishment, in order to encourage these children to adopt the *desirable* elements of middle-class culture.

Concerning rewards offered to lower-class groups, Allison Davis says that "our educational system, which next to the family is the most effective agency in teaching good work habits to middle-class people, is largely ineffective and unrealistic with underprivileged groups."

"Education," he says, "fails to motivate such workers because our schools and our society both lack *real rewards* to offer underprivileged groups. Neither lower-class children nor adults will work hard in school or on the job just to please the teacher or boss. They are not going to learn to be ambitious, to be conscientious and to study hard, as if school and work were a fine character-building game, which one plays just for the sake of playing." [37]

It would seem, then, that if we want to influence the behavior of lower-income groups, reduce delinquency, and raise achievement levels, we must learn new ways of reaching these groups, and we must provide rules to which they can adjust and rewards which will stimulate their interest in school.

Rewards and Punishment

Perhaps all human behavior is controlled by systems of rewards and punishments. We work because we know that if we do we will win favor in our family and in society, and, perhaps more important, that we will get a paycheck at the end of the week. We know, in other words, that we will be rewarded for our work.

Some of us, perhaps, refrain from injuring other people or stealing their property only because we know that, unless we do, we will probably be punished for our behavior.

While rewards and punishments both affect behavior, rewards are almost always preferable to punishments as a means of control. Rewards are positive and punishment negative. Rewards stimulate desire and voluntary participation, while punishment stimulates fear and often hatred, rebelliousness, and delinquency.

Moreover, prolonged punishment tends to discourage children and to undermine their confidence in themselves and in the world. In brief these excessive and continuous punishments tend either to destroy a child's self-esteem or to create in him a desire to destroy others. In either case the results are tragic for the individual and for society.

The schools therefore should aim at controlling, or disciplining, students by rewards rather than by punishment. Very often they do. The trouble is, however, that, though the schools offer many rewards, these rewards are not open to all students. In most cases the schools deliberately restrict the number of students who can win important rewards, limiting, for example, the percentage of students who can get A's or who can be admitted to special programs. Because of these restrictions a great many children are not able to win rewards. Moreover, many don't know what the rewards are worth and so do not *seek* to win them. The end result is that, in general, upper-income groups win most of the rewards and lower-income groups get most of the punishment.

School rewards are put too far out of the reach of lower-income students. They are not equipped to win rewards in competition with more privileged groups, and since there are not enough rewards to go around, they usually give up. In many cases their reaction is "I didn't want them anyhow, I'm not interested and I'm not even going to try." Often the reaction is anger, loss of confidence and self-esteem, and withdrawal from school life.

While a great many lower-income students pretend they do not want school rewards (knowing they can't get them anyway), many genuinely do not seek these rewards. They have little natural interest in them, and they have no knowledge of what the rewards are worth (what can you do with a gold star that's worth the effort of getting it?)

Perhaps the biggest prize and the most coveted reward offered by the schools is the possibility of a college education. Going to college usually means getting a better job than average, with higher pay, better working conditions, greater security and prestige, and a generally richer, fuller life.

Most lower-income children do not understand this. They cannot appraise the value of a college education nor do they understand that students must begin to prepare for college even in the elementary school grades. Perhaps even more to the point, they do not realize that a college education could ever be *possible* for them.

This is a reward, then, which they do not seek or respond to. Under present conditions they would be more likely to respond to an offer of candy or a trip to a ball game. They know that candy is good—but what good is a college education?

The truth is that lower-income children have never been "sold" on the value of a college education. Education beyond high school, in fact, is rarely put to them as a possibility. Until students come right up to the finishing line (at high-school graduation time) the importance or possibility of a continuing education is seldom even mentioned in lower-income schools. Upper-income students usually know about college through their family or friends, and they are driven to perform well in school in order to win this coveted prize, a college education (preferably at a prestige school). Lower-income students don't compete because they usually do not know what the prize is, what it is worth, or how one goes about getting it.

Some of the rewards and punishments offered in Big City schools—failure rates, admissions to Detention School and Ungraded Classes, and selections for "gifted"-child programs have been discussed. Such rewards as admission to college-preparatory curriculums, "ability" groupings, college attendance, and special prizes and awards will be discussed later. Several varieties of school rewards and punishments were not within the scope of this study, and so we must turn to other sources for information about them.

S. Abrahamson studied 705 students in the seventh, eighth, and ninth grades in six different communities. He found that, of this group, upper-class students got most of the rewards, while lower-class students got most of the punishment. Some of his findings follow.[38]

Grades: Good report-card marks are one of the chief rewards offered by the schools, and poor marks one of the chief punishments, though not a very effective one. Abrahamson found that the distribution of good grades (A and B) and poor grades (D and E) was as follows. (The numbers in parentheses indicate the number of students who *should* have received these grades, according to population in each income group.)

CLASS	A & B GRADES	D & E GRADES
"Upper middle class"	343 (216)	19 (75)
"Lower lower class"	48 (147)	136 (51)

Prizes: Of the eighteen winners of American Legion Awards for outstanding citizenship, fourteen were of "upper-middle-class" background and the other four of "lower-middle-class" background. No "lower-class" students received awards—even though one-third of all students were of the "lower class."

Social Acceptance: Studies of early adolescence show, Abrahamson says, that acceptance by other students is a powerful motivational force, but according to this research most of this acceptance is bestowed on students who are already highly motivated. Students were rated on the Ohio Social Acceptance Scale, with high and low scores distributed as follows (again, the numbers in parentheses indicate the rightful or proportionate share of these scores).

CLASS	HIGH SCORES	LOW SCORES
"Upper middle class"	45 (22)	27 (48)
"Lower lower class"	3 (19)	62 (40)

Offices Held and Extracurricular Activities: Almost all elected student offices were held by "middle-class" students. No "lower-lower-class" student held any office. "Upper-lower-class" students held less than one-third of their share of offices. At the same time, "upper-middle-

class" students held about three times their share of these
elected offices.

Abrahamson says about extracurricular activities: "Participation in extracurricular activities in a school program
acts as a reward in that the students involved in the activities develop a deeper sense of appreciation for school,
a higher level of morale, and a keen feeling of sharing in
the school program. Again, the evidence was obvious. The
higher the social class background of the students, the
more they tended to participate in extracurricular activities."

Favors and Punishment by the Teachers: Perhaps student preference for "upper-class" students, as shown in
elections, was simply a reflection of teacher preference.
Abrahamson found that, "according to the teachers themselves, there was a tendency to favor the students from
higher social class backgrounds. The teachers indicated
that the students of higher social class backgrounds were
chosen more often for little favors—running errands,
monitoring, committee chairman, and the like—than
were the other children. Obversely, when it came to
handing out disciplinary measures there was a tendency
for the students of lower social class backgrounds to receive much more than their share according to the ratings of the teachers."

Thus in Abrahamson's six communities most of the good
report-card marks, prizes, social acceptance, elected student offices, extracurricular club memberships, and teachers' favors went to "upper-class" students, while a dispro-
portionate share of the punishment went to "lower-class"
students.

Among the discoveries made by August B. Hollingshead about rewards and punishment in Elmtown high school were the following:[39]

Out-of-Class Aid to Students: While only 27 per cent of students in Elmtown's second-highest class were reported at one time or another for poor or failing work, 63 per cent received aid outside of class from their teachers. Among the "lowest-class" students, 92 per cent were reported for poor or failing work, yet only 8 per cent received aid outside of class.

Family Influence: Concerning the use of "family" pressure on the schools, subtle or overt, Hollingshead says: "The two upper classes generally assume that good grades, school prizes, student offices, and prominence in scholastic affairs are their natural due. New teachers soon learn . . . 'who is who' and what one should or should not do to avoid trouble. Teachers, if they are successful act judiciously in their relations with the children of the powerful; on appropriate occasions they look the other way."

Discipline: During the course of Hollingshead's study the school set up a new procedure for dealing with tardy students. According to the new rules, any student coming late would be required to sit in the study hall for one hour after school, no excuses accepted. After the adoption of these rules the superintendent of schools made this comment, off the record: "You cannot make a rule like that stick in this town. There are students who simply cannot be sent to detention. Their families will not stand for it. I look for trouble from this."

Not long after the rule was adopted, says Hollingshead, "Frank Stone, Jr. (from the highest class), parked his father's Cadillac in front of the high school at a quarter after eight, climbed out leisurely, picked up his notebook, and walked into the office and casually remarked, 'I guess I'm late again.' "

At the superintendent's intervention, Frank Stone, Jr., was not sent to detention for his tardiness. "This practically ended uniform enforcement of the new detention rule," according to Hollingshead. Thereafter the upper-class students "flouted it on the least pretext. However, it was enforced more rigidly for many others."

Three weeks after the Frank Stone, Jr., incident, "Boney" Johnson (from the second-lowest class) came late one morning. As Boney walked into the office the principal was sitting at his desk. Before Boney could say a word he barked in a sarcastic tone, "So my pretty boy is late again! I suppose it took you half an hour to put on that clean shirt and green tie! Ha, you have your pants pressed today! I suppose you took a bath last night too. New shoes, and they're shined."

The principal told Boney he would have to go to detention. After the boy had left the room the principal said, "Now there's a hot one. He's one of our wise guys. He thinks he's a hotshot. His old man is a laborer out at the fertilizer plant, and the kid thinks he's someone, umph! He'll be on the WPA if they have one twenty years from now. There's one guy I'm going to see put in detention."

Boney refused to go to detention, and because of his difficulties with the principal following this refusal, Boney quit school.

The Child and Environs

Disturbed Children

We have been searching for explanations of the high failure and delinquency rates found among lower-income youths. We have seen that the "middle-class" culture of the school tends to alienate these youths, and that the rewards-and-punishments system of the school tends even further to exclude and discourage them.

Now let us turn from the causes of maladjustment to possible remedies (not cures, since effective cures perhaps depend on changes in the whole structure of the schools and society). Specifically, what first-aid services are provided in Big City schools for "problem" children and for children who are otherwise disturbed and unable to perform in school? We are not referring to services such as Detention School, Ungraded Classes, and special schools, none of which could be described as "remedial," except in so far as they reduce the problems of the schools. Rather, we are interested in: What is being done to reduce the problems of delinquent and disturbed children? The unavoidable response to this question is that apparently very little is being done.

The only "treatment" services offered are under the jurisdiction of the Psychological Clinic of the board of education. This clinic performs several vital functions in the schools. It administers the Visiting Teacher program, a social casework program that provides special teachers to "visit" the schools and homes of problem children. It is in charge of all psychological testing services for disturbed and problem children. It handles all the aptitude and IQ tests given in the city's schools.

Unfortunately this department refused to release any information about its operations, even when reminded that the taxpaying public is entitled to know what is being done. The reason given for the refusal: fear that such information might be used to criticize the conduct of the department's affairs.

Information from other sources indicates that there is a very lengthy waiting list for the psychological tests given by the clinic and that the list is longest in low-income areas. These diagnostic tests are the beginning of treatment for disturbed children, and without them little progress can be made in solving their emotional problems.

Treatment services for disturbed children are also reported to be totally inadequate. In fact very little treatment is offered. A seriously disturbed child, if he is lucky, will be referred to the clinic for testing. He will then be put on the waiting list for diagnostic testing. If his luck holds out long enough, he will be tested. If it is found that he needs treatment, he will be referred to other community agencies or to specialists in private practice. If his parents cannot afford treatment from a private specialist, he must apply to a community agency. But the waiting lists for services in these agencies are also extremely long, and the child will be remarkably fortunate if he receives adequate treatment before it is too late.

The clinic employs only one psychiatrist, who works as a consultant on a part-time basis. The clinic also employs thirty-eight Visiting Teachers who do social casework with pre-delinquents and children with "personality disturbances." Since there are nearly 300 schools in the city, the work of these teachers is spread very thin. Limited as it is, the Visiting Teacher program is practically the only treatment service offered to disturbed children. The program was originally set up to deal with delinquency, and this is still its main focus. The quiet children, the ones with hidden problems that cause no disturbance in the school, are seldom given much attention.

Aside from these bare facts, very little is known about the work of the Psychological Clinic. The clinic is a key agency for the low-income child. As the following material on the disturbed child indicates, the importance of its work cannot be overestimated.

While preparing this study, the author was challenged by a well-informed university instructor, who asked: "Do you really believe that kids in upper-income groups are happier than kids in lower-income groups?" Knowing something first-hand about the taboos that inhibit upper-status groups, he apparently assumed, as a great many others do, that lower-income groups must be freer and happier. Many individuals in these groups, after all, have a reputation for being "happy-go-lucky" and rather carefree.

Luckily the author did not have to meet this challenge unaided. A carefully documented response had already been prepared by James V. Mitchell, Jr.[40]

Mitchell gave a personality test to 44,000 children in the Midwest. He then analyzed the answers of children of "high" and "low" status to the test questions. If "high status" is taken to mean the upper-income groups referred to by the university instructor, then we can see that upper-income students are much happier than lower-income students, no matter how the term "happy" is defined.

This study provides so revealing a portrait of the personalities and problems of high- and low-status children that we include a rather full account of it here. Responses are included from both the fifth and the seventh grades. Most of the items at these two grade levels are different. A few are the same. Some of these are quite significant; for example, in the fifth grade 42 per cent of low-status children said they wished their father or mother had a better job. In the seventh grade, 61 per cent expressed this wish, indicating that students become more aware of jobs and social class factors as they grow older.

The numbers in the right-hand columns indicate the percentage of students answering "yes" to the questions.

Fifth Graders

QUESTION	"YES" ANSWERS	
	LOW STATUS	HIGH STATUS
1. Do you get excited when things go wrong?	77%	46%
2. Do you wish that your father (or mother) had a better job?	42	8
3. Do your classmates and friends usually feel that they know more than you do?	62	27
4. May you usually do what you want to during your spare time?	54	92
5. Are you allowed to do most of the things you want to?	42	85
6. Do you often think that nobody likes you?	62	19
7. Do you have just a few friends?	42	4

FIFTH GRADERS (*continued*)

QUESTION	"YES" ANSWERS	
	LOW STATUS	HIGH STATUS
8. Are people often so unkind or unfair that it makes you feel bad?	62	15
9. Are your studies or your life so dull that you often think about many other things?	46	15
10. Do you often have sneezing spells?	50	8
11. Do you often have bad dreams?	58	23
12. Do you bite your fingernails often?	54	23
13. Do you often find you are not hungry at meal time?	65	27
14. Do you often feel sick at your stomach?	54	23
15. Do people often act so badly that you have to be mean or nasty to them?	46	8
16. Is it hard to make people remember how well you can do things?	46	15
17. Do you like both of your parents about the same?	65	92
18. Does someone at home pick on you much of the time?	42	0
19. Do you think there are too few interesting places near your home?	54	19

SEVENTH GRADERS

QUESTION	"YES" ANSWERS	
	LOW STATUS	HIGH STATUS
1. Do you wish your father or mother had a better job?	61%	15%
2. Do people often think you cannot do things very well?	54	27
3. Do you have a chance to see many new things?	61	96
4. Do your folks often stop you from going around with your friends?	39	11
5. Do you often think that nobody likes you?	46	11

Seventh Graders (*continued*)

QUESTION	"YES" ANSWERS	
	LOW STATUS	HIGH STATUS
6. Do you often think of many things that are dangerous?	86	56
7. Do you often meet people who are so mean that you hate them?	68	11
8. Are you often greatly discouraged about many things that are important to you?	82	26
9. Are people often so unkind or unfair that it makes you feel bad?	57	26
10. Do your friends or classmates often say or do things that hurt your feelings?	61	30
11. Do people often try to cheat you or do mean things to you?	46	11
12. Are people often mean or unfair to you?	43	11
13. Do you bite your fingernails often?	50	21
14. Do you often find that you are not hungry at meal time?	50	21
15. Do you take cold easily?	36	11
16. Do you often feel sick at your stomach?	50	7
17. Do you often have dizzy spells?	32	7
18. Is it hard for you to talk to people as soon as you meet them?	57	18
19. Do people often ask you to do such hard or foolish things that you won't do them?	61	25
20. Do you often have to "fuss" or "act up" to get your rights?	36	4
21. Do many of the children get along with the teacher much better than you do?	50	15

Commenting on this personality portrait, Mitchell says: "The Low Status child is more likely to feel that people in his environment dislike him, are taking advantage of him, or are treating him unfairly, and his typical reaction is resentment and hostility."

Responses to these questions tell us a very great deal about why delinquency and emotional disturbance are so much more common among low-status children. They also tell us why psychological services are so important for these children.

Judith Krugman also studied a group of lower-class, "culturally deprived" children. She says: "When one knows something about the problems these children face in their lives, one cannot help but be impressed that they are able to achieve even as well as they do. Their cultural limitations might not limit learning so much if there were compensating conditions. However, when environmental pressures seriously weaken enthusiasm, confidence, and self-assurance, school functioning is adversely affected." [41]

Krugman claims that many of these culturally deprived children have been injured by their experiences inside of school and out, with the result that they: question their own worth; feel inferior, particularly in the school situation; fear new situations more than they feel their challenge; desire to cling tenaciously to the familiar; have many feelings of guilt and shame; have limited trust in adults; respond with trigger-like reactions to apparently minor frustrations.

These personality injuries, she says, seem to weigh most heavily on the boys, and the "profound lack of self-respect is most crippling." About 30 per cent of all the children in the study group, she claims, had emotional problems that required specialized treatment. A still larger percentage were noted by the teacher to be "restless, nervous, shy, or emotionally disturbed" at some time or other during their school life. About one-third of the total group were very thin or pale.

Despite the urgent need of lower-income students for psychological attention, apparently very little is known in Big City about the emotional and personal problems of these or any other students. The only systematic effort that has been made to investigate these problems (so far as could be ascertained) was a testing program conducted by the department of educational research. Though such tests are more the responsibility of the Psychological Clinic, this research department gave the Mooney Problem Check List to numbers of students in Big City schools.

The Mooney Check List is very much like the California Test of Personality used by Mitchell in the study previously described. On this quiz the children were asked to check the problems that were troubling them at the moment. Such tests can be used very constructively by teachers and administrators to guide students, to understand them better, and to help solve their personal problems. They can also be used to determine which schools and areas of the city are in greatest need of counseling and psychological services.

The remarkable fact, however, is that, though the Mooney test was administered on a large scale throughout the city, the results were never tabulated. The tests were given in the schools, sent to the department of origin, and there they still lie, uncounted and ignored. We do not know why. Some of the personnel in this department were very reluctant to release information, and this was among the items of information that were not forthcoming.

In this failure to tabulate or make use of these test

results we can find perhaps no better testimony, silent though it is, to the general apathy and inaction which characterize the attitude of the schools and the community toward emotionally disturbed children.

We have been discussing the school performance of various income groups in Big City—their achievement scores, IQ levels, admissions to "gifted"-child programs, Ungraded Classes and Detention School—as well as the emotional problems of lower-income, delinquency-prone youths.

Now let us give the schools a brief rest while we move on to subjects which are not so highly charged. Before doing that, it should be repeated that whatever criticisms are made of the schools here, and they may seem harsh at times, are not directed at individuals or at the schools of Big City specifically. The problems of lower-income students have been seriously neglected, not only in Big City but apparently in many areas throughout the country, and, though schools everywhere have many problems and limited resources, this is one problem they cannot any longer afford to ignore or neglect.

Pupil Turnover

Teachers who have taught in low-income schools know that the turnover of pupils in these schools is so great that it is difficult to keep permanent seating charts or to know who is in class at the moment.

Because of this and a number of related factors, the teacher's job is harder and less rewarding in lower-income schools. She cannot establish much continuity in her classes —in subject matter or in relations with her students. She

must spend much of her time getting to know her new
students and introducing them to the work they are doing.
And, with all this effort, it is difficult for her to feel she has
accomplished much. She cannot see the results of her
efforts in front of her; they have moved elsewhere, and she
must start over again.

Why are turnover rates so high in the lower-income
areas? Many of these areas house new arrivals to the city,
numbers of whom come from the South and, lacking skills,
find work in the lowest-paying jobs. When these families
accumulate a little money, they tend to move to better
residential areas; some of them return to their homes,
especially during periods of tight employment.

Also, people in low-income areas are usually renters, not
home-owners, and so they are not "attached" to their
housing or their neighborhoods. Add this detachment to
the high incidence of broken homes and the fact that low-
income individuals are often "at large" occupationally
and emotionally, and we get some insight into the causes
of high transiency rates in lower-income schools.

The turnover rates shown in this table include all students who either entered or left a school during one
semester. (These are percentages of the total number of
students enrolled in each income group.)

INCOME GROUP	TURNOVER PERCENTAGES
I ($3000—)	49.0%
II ($5000—)	46.7
III ($7000—)	21.5
IV ($9000—)	16.7

Thus, in the lowest-income group there was a pupil
turnover of almost 50 per cent during one semester. The

rate in the lowest-income group is *three* times as great as the rate in the highest-income group.

But that is not all. Among the minor income groups, group 1 ($3500 income) had a turnover rate of 59.6 per cent, while group 26 (the highest-income group—$11,055) had a rate of only 13.1 per cent. This amounts to a difference of 46.5 per cent.

Obviously, this constant movement makes it difficult for children to do well in school. These transient youths have no roots in their community; they are not known in school or in their neighborhoods, and they have difficulty establishing much continuity in their school work.

Turnover rates in Big City are broken down into various categories, among which are the following:

Losses—Under or Over Compulsory School Age: During the semester there were 398 drop-outs in the elementary schools. It is commonly assumed that all drop-outs occur at the high-school level since law prohibits students from leaving school in Big City before they are sixteen, at which time they are normally in the tenth grade.

Most of these drop-outs, of course, were at least age sixteen, though still in elementary school. An unspecified number, however, were under sixteen. The distribution of these drop-outs (per 10,000 students) was as follows.

INCOME GROUP	DROP-OUTS
I ($3000—)	15.5
II ($5000—)	3.0
III ($7000—)	1.5
IV ($9000—)	.7

We see from these figures that the drop-out rate in group I is 22 *times* greater than the rate in group IV.

Moved—Cannot Locate: The following figures show that in lower-income groups there is an extremely dispro- portionate number of students who move out of the school area and cannot be located. The community ties of lower- income groups are so slight that families literally disap- pear from their neighborhoods, leaving no word and no forwarding address with teachers or neighbors. (Again, these figures show the number of students per 10,000 in each income group.)

INCOME GROUP	UNLOCATED STUDENTS
I ($3000—)	73.4
II ($5000—)	59.5
III ($7000—)	7.9
IV ($9000—)	2.1

Losses Due to Illness: During the semester 166 students left school because of long-term illness, with the following income distribution.

INCOME GROUP	LOSSES DUE TO ILLNESS
I ($3000—)	10.7
II ($5000—)	8.4
III ($7000—)	8.4
IV ($9000—)	5.3

The rate (per 10,000 students) of losses due to illness is therefore *twice* as great in group I as in group IV.

Attendance

School attendance is also related to income. The worst at- tendance record (among the minor groups) was found in the lowest-income group, where the attendance rate during the week under examination was 87.7 per cent.

The best record was found in the highest-income group, where the attendance rate was 93.8 per cent. Thus in group 26 there were 6.1 per cent more students attending school during the week than in group 1.

The distribution by major income groups was as follows.

INCOME GROUP	ATTENDANCE RATE
I ($3000—)	90.4%
II ($5000—)	90.9
III ($7000—)	92.3
IV ($9000—)	93.2

Sickness and Medical Problems

Lower-income children often have trouble in school because of sickness and health problems. They are much more likely than upper-income children to be sick or diseased or to suffer from some chronic ailment that goes undetected or untreated. This is probably a result of the fact that lower-income children are not as well cared for as upper-income children. They are not so well fed, their housing conditions are more conducive to epidemic disease, and they do not as often get proper medical attention and care.

Rheumatic fever is not an illness that has been associated in the public mind with income levels or with the "ability to buy medical care." Health department reports indicate, however, that there is a close association between this disabling illness and family income in Big City. The distribution of rheumatic-fever victims (per 10,000 students) during the course of a year was as follows.

INCOME GROUP	RHEUMATIC-FEVER RATE
I ($3000—)	7.9
II ($5000—)	6.4
III ($7000—)	4.8
IV ($9000—)	2.6

Thus, the rate is *three* times higher in group I than in group IV. Rheumatic fever is often a consequence of untreated "strep" throat, and children in lower-income groups are not likely to be taken to a doctor for a sore throat.

The following figures show that diphtheria (a disease which was epidemic in Big City in recent years) takes a disproportionately heavy toll of children in group I. At the opposite end of the income ladder, the rate in group IV was zero. Per 10,000 students, these rates were:

INCOME GROUP	DIPHTHERIA RATE
I ($3000—)	15.1
II ($5000—)	1.4
III ($7000—)	.9
IV ($9000—)	0

Diphtheria, it appears, is more closely related to income in Big City than tuberculosis, the traditional disease of poverty. The TB rate, per 10,000 students, was as follows.

INCOME GROUP	TB RATE
I ($3000—)	6.8
II ($5000—)	3.4
III ($7000—)	.6
IV ($9000—)	0

As with diphtheria, the rate in group IV was zero. The rate in group I was twice as high as the rate in group II, and more than eleven times as high as in group III.

Schools in Big City do not require that children entering the first grade receive smallpox and diphtheria-tetanus vaccinations, but they strongly urge it. These vaccinations are supposed to be administered by private physicians and paid for out of private funds. Where great need is apparent, free vaccinations are sometimes provided in the schools. Families on public welfare can also get some financial assistance if they take their children to private physicians for these vaccinations.

Despite these aids, about 21 per cent of all children in group I did not receive smallpox vaccinations, and about 19 per cent did not receive diphtheria-tetanus shots.

On the other hand, in group IV only 4 per cent of all children did not receive smallpox vaccinations, and only 1.7 per cent did not receive diphtheria-tetanus shots. The percentages that did *not* receive vaccinations were the following.

INCOME GROUP	SMALLPOX	DIPHTHERIA-TETANUS
I ($3000—)	20.9%	18.9%
II ($5000—)	16.4	12.3
III ($7000—)	8.4	4.0
IV ($9000—)	3.9	1.7

The situation is even worse in the small, minor income groups. In one of these groups (the second-lowest in income), 30.8 per cent of all students did not receive smallpox vaccinations, and 27.5 per cent did not receive diphtheria-tetanus shots. Little wonder, then, that so many lower-income children have contracted diphtheria.

Medical examinations for children entering first grade are also urged but not required. Obviously if a child is ill or if he suffers from some undiagnosed sight, hearing, or speech defect, his chances of doing well in school are greatly reduced. The doctor's examination is a certificate of good health.

Despite the importance of these examinations, almost *half* of all children in group I did not receive them. In group IV, only 7 per cent did not receive them.

HEALTH DIVISION, IN ORDER OF INCREASING INCOME GROUP	STUDENTS NOT RECEIVING HEALTH EXAMINATIONS
A	55.2%
B	57.2
C	35.4
D	45.5
E	37.4
F	36.3
G	45.8
H	17.6
I	21.5
J	11.6
K	12.1
L	12.5
M	10.4
N	7.9
O	8.5
P	4.5

The disparities found in the minor income groups are even greater. The minor group rates are included here in order to provide a more detailed picture of the kind of medical care various income groups are receiving. (The minor group divisions are different from those used previously because, of necessity, they are based on large health department divisions rather than on individual schools. If information had been available on separate schools, the differences among income groups would have been even greater than they are. Still the differences are substantial, as these figures show.)

The major group distributions were:

INCOME GROUP	STUDENTS NOT RECEIVING HEALTH EXAMINATIONS
I	49.3%
II	36.5
III	13.6
IV	7.0

More evidence that low-income children do not get the kind of medical attention they need comes from the records of school nurses. According to nurses' reports, lower-income children are much less likely to receive medical attention recommended by school nurses than are upper-income children.

School nurses do some diagnostic work in the schools. They examine eyes, ears, throat, etc., and when they discover a defect they refer the child to his "own private physician" for treatment. Very often, because the family does not have or cannot afford a family physician, the child is not treated and continues in school despite his recognized handicap. The following figures show the distribution of these untreated defects during a one-year period. (These divisions are based on school nursing areas. Again, the differences among income groups would probably have been much greater if information had been available on individual schools.)

NURSING DIVISIONS (IN ORDER OF INCREASING INCOME)	CHILDREN WITH DIAGNOSED DEFECTS WHO RECEIVED NO TREATMENT		
	TOTAL DEFECTS	VISION	HEARING
1	32.5%	31.1%	53.2%
2	31.7	37.6	41.0
3	31.3	29.8	42.5
4	29.8	29.1	39.8
5	15.5	13.5	34.6

Thus in group 1, 32.5 per cent of all diagnosed defects (including heart, vision, hearing, etc.) went untreated. In group 5, only 15.5 per cent of all defects went untreated. The percentage of untreated defects in group 1 therefore is more than *twice* what it is in group 5.

The difference between the two groups in untreated vision defects is even greater. The difference in untreated hearing defects is not so great; still, more than half of all children in group 1 with hearing defects have received no treatment.

Since good vision and hearing are essential to school success, it seems quite urgent that the schools devise new ways of dealing with the problem of untreated defects and with the unmet health needs of lower-income groups. Together with the Department of Health, the schools have a clear responsibility to provide, by one means or another, all necessary medical care for children whose families do not or cannot provide it.

Vital Statistics

The statistics in Table 7, concerning birth and death rates in Big City (adults included), come from the Department of Health. (Again, of necessity, income divisions are different from preceding ones.)

TABLE 7. Big City Birth and Death Rates

	GROUP I (BELOW $6000)	GROUP II ($6000—)	GROUP III ($7000—)	GROUP IV ($8000—)
Birth rate (per 1000 population)	22.2	20.2	17.2	16.9
Death rate (per 1000 population)	8.9	7.7	6.5	6.5
Maternal mortality (per 1000 live births)	.53	1.02	.31	0
Infant mortality (per 1000 live births)	38.2	28.1	20.2	19.2
Heart death rate (per 100,000)	335.9	307.8	279.3	281.1
Cancer death rate (per 100,000)	142.7	134.3	122.4	142.0
Accident death rate (per 100,000)	35.4	31.8	24.6	17.8
Pneumonia death rate (per 100,000)	38.6	19.8	12.6	8.8

Thus both birth and death rates are highest in the lowest-income groups. The maternal mortality rate is zero in group IV, and unexplainably highest in group II. Infant mortality is almost twice as great in group I as in group IV. Heart and cancer death rates are somewhat higher in the lowest-income groups, with the rates in group IV unusually high in both cases. The accident death rate is almost twice as high in group I as in group IV. The pneumonia death rate in group I is more than four times as high as the rate in group IV.

The Parent

Parent Groups

In a very real sense parents are responsible for the success or failure of their children in school. The child is a product of his family and class background just as his parents are of theirs. Very often the child is simply a reflection of parental attitudes, values, skills, and levels of understanding. Because of this, the schools must seek the help and cooperation of parents if they want to change the behavior of students.

How successfully is the job of reaching parents being done in Big City? The following chart gives us some idea; it shows the rate of parent-group memberships per 100 students enrolled in each income group.

INCOME	INCOME GROUP	RATE OF PARENT MEMBERSHIPS
$3000—	1	11.9
	2	5.1
	3	7.6
	4	12.2
	5	16.1
$5000—	6	3.8
	7	6.9
	8	13.6
	9	12.7
	10	9.6
	11	12.2
	12	11.4
	13	11.8
	14	16.2
	15	18.8

INCOME	INCOME GROUP	RATE OF PARENT MEMBERSHIPS
$7000—	16	32.9
	17	34.5
	18	40.7
	19	37.2
	20	57.5
	21	58.4
	22	31.3
	23	51.1
$9000—	24	69.5
	25	48.3
	26	103.3

The distribution by major income groups was as follows.

INCOME GROUP	PARENT MEMBERSHIP
I ($3000—)	10.1
II ($5000—)	12.3
III ($7000—)	42.3
IV ($9000—)	73.8

These parent membership figures include *both* parents. That is why there are more parent members in group 26 than there are students in this group.

In group 6 the rate is only 3.8. This means that the difference between group 6 and group 26 rates is 100.

It will also be noted that the rate in group IV is *seven times* higher than the rate in group I. One of the most striking facts revealed in this table is the sharp difference between groups in the lower-income half (below $7000 income) and those in the upper-income half. No group in the lower-income half has a rate as high as 20.0; no group in the upper-income half has a rate of less than 30.0.

These figures indicate an extremely imbalanced distribution of parent memberships. Parents whose children have most trouble in school—that is, lower-income parents —are least likely to join a school-parent group.

In general, lower-income adults tend to be non-joiners and non-participants. This is especially true, apparently, when it comes to joining school groups. Many explanations have been offered for this. Lower-income individuals rarely feel at ease in social groups. Since they seldom have much group or social experience, they do not have very highly developed social skills. And it is the absence of these skills that often prevents them from raising their income and social status levels.

What is perhaps most obvious about the social behavior of many lower-income people is that they are not able to carry on the kind of small-talk conversation required in social situations. They cannot talk to the teacher. They cannot talk to strangers. Even when seated at a dinner table, where conversation is a social necessity, they usually cannot meet minimum conversation needs. Nor do they go out of their way to meet people and engage them in conversation, as upper-income individuals do, and so they never develop the "contacts" that lead to social, economic —and often academic—success.

They seldom shake hands. They almost never make introductions, even in their own homes. They are seldom confident, extroverted, aggressive, as upper-income individuals usually are, and they tend to be timid and uneasy around people they don't know—especially the people of status and influence who could "help" them and their children.

Such social behavior is certainly understandable. When people do not have the money, the know-how, or the housing facilities to "entertain" at home, when they do not join clubs and groups where they meet people, when they do not "belong," they have little opportunity to develop skill at conversation, hand-shaking, introductions, and the various social graces required to win-friends-and-influence-people.

In school, they are likely to feel more ill-at-ease than elsewhere. In this setting, where memories of past experiences are usually less than pleasant, they are likely to feel uncomfortable and self-conscious about their dress and the way they talk and their general behavior. What is more, lacking confidence in themselves and remembering their own school days, they often fear that, if they visit the school, the teacher will scold them or criticize their children's behavior as teachers once criticized their own. This fear is sometimes unfounded, but not always. Teachers sometimes *do* scold and criticize parents.

The following passage from Harriette Arnow's *The Doll-maker* describes, much better than statistics could, what can and does occasionally happen between teacher and lower-income parent on school visiting day. The parent in this case is a Southern woman who has recently come North with her family.[42]

It was getting late, the children marching homeward through the halls, before she reached the one room she dreaded—Mrs. Whittle's. . . .

She waited a moment longer, then cleared her throat and said, "Miz Whittle." The woman opened the cupboard door and gave a slight backward nod as if to indicate that she had heard. . . .

Gertie moved a step nearer and stood by the desk. The woman was now taking a dark green felt hat from a shelf and did not look around when Gertie said, "I come to talk to you about my youngen—boy."

Mrs. Whittle, with a crinkling hiss of paper, was removing the hat from a green paper sack. "You'll have to hurry," she said, her voice somehow matching the paper. "It's late and I've been teaching and talking to mothers all afternoon."

"Th slip my youngens brung home said th teachers ud talk to us atter school," Gertie said, speaking with difficulty, choked up at being forced to speak to the woman's back. . . .

"Well, what is the matter? Did your child fail to pass? A percentage do, you know."

"No, he passed," Gertie said, fighting to keep her voice smooth. "But—but you're his . . ." She had forgotten the name, the kind of teacher. "You've got him more'n th other teachers, an you'll keep on a haven him an . . ."

"Are you trying to say that I'm his home-room teacher?" Mrs. Whittle asked, drawing on a glove.

Gertie nodded.

"Well, what is the matter?" She was smoothing the drawn-on gloves finger by finger now.

"He—he don't seem to be a doen so good—not in his home room. He ain't happy; he don't like school, an I thought mebbe . . ."

Her words, though halting and stumbling as they were, caused Mrs. Whittle to glance up from the second glove, and for the first time the two women looked at each other. Mrs. Whittle smiled, the red mouth widening below the old woman's angry glaring eyes. "And of course it's his teacher's fault your child is unhappy. Now just what do you expect me to do to make him happy?"

"That's what I come to ask you," Gertie said. "He kinda likes his other classes, an back home he was . . ."

"Back home," Mrs. Whittle said, as if she hated the words, her voice low, hissing, like a thin whip coming hard through the air, but not making much noise. "You hill—southerners who come here, don't you realize before you come that it will be a great change for your children? For the better, of course, but still a change. You bring them up here in time of war to an overcrowded part of the city and it makes for an overcrowded school. Don't you realize," she went on, looking again at Gertie, looking at her as if she alone were responsible for it all, "that until they built this wartime housing —I presume you live there—I never had more than thirty-two children in my section—and only one section." She opened her purse. "Now I have two sections—two home rooms, one in the morning with forty-three children, one in the afternoon with forty-two—many badly adjusted like your own—yet you expect me to make your child happy in spite of . . ." Words seemed inadequate, and she was silent while she reached for her purse.

"But I've got three more in school, an they git along an—"

"What did you say your name was?"

"Nevels. My boy's name is Reuben. Maybe you don't recollect him, but—"

"I don't what?" And she frowned as she might have at a child giving the wrong answer.

" 'Recollect,' I said," Gertie answered.

"Does that mean 'remember'?"

This encounter is not necessarily typical, but it happens often enough to make parents like Gertie very apprehensive about their appearances at school. Of course there are numbers of excellent, devoted teachers in these schools, but the Whittles are there too, though in declining numbers, it is hoped.

Lower-income parents often give the wrong answers in school; that is why they stay away. Involving them in school affairs will require much more than written invitations or a sharp complaining phone call from the principal about their child's behavior. It will require warm encouragement, school activities that are interesting, and programs that make sense. Most of all it will require energetic organizers, teachers who can talk with uneducated people without looking down their noses, and lots of hard work.

Are Big City schools trying hard enough to reach lower-income parents? Some feel very strongly that they are not. Such matters, however, were not within the scope of this investigation; further research on the subject seems to be in order.

Much improvement in school-parent relations is obviously possible, judging by the preceding tables, which indicate that some lower-income schools have been more successful than others in their work with parents. If good work can be done in some schools, it can be done in others.

In recognition of the complexity of the problem, it should be said that parents, when activated, can be a source of trouble for teachers and administrators. They take up the staff's time; they interfere in the school's affairs; they protest and they criticize. These problems, however, are the inevitable companions of awakened parent interest. They are very good symptoms—not bad ones. They indicate that the patient is alive and making progress, however irritating it may be to others. Progress is usually accompanied by some degree of trouble and confusion; by definition it involves changes in the status quo and often disruption. But, whatever mild or even serious discomfort it may cause to some, it would appear to be worth it in the long run.

Extension Classes for Adults

Most adult evening classes and community group meetings are held in high-school rather than elementary-school
buildings and will therefore be dealt with later, along with
other high-school activities. "Extension" classes are among
the very few elementary-school services provided for adults.
These classes are offered in various subjects at the request
of community groups, and they are held in homes, various
community buildings, and the schools themselves. As the
following figures show, this program is conducted almost
exclusively for the two upper-income groups. (Figures here
indicate number of classes per ten schools in each income
group.)

INCOME GROUP	NUMBER OF CLASSES
I ($3000—)	.30
II ($5000—)	.93
III ($7000—)	4.71
IV ($9000—)	11.58

The Quality of Education

A further examination of services offered to students in
Big City schools—specifically, class size, school overcrowding, teaching staff, and, at some length, the quality of
school buildings and facilities—reveals the following facts
about social class as it relates to school services.

Class Size

It is widely assumed that class size is smaller in lower-
income areas, where students tend to be harder to handle

and in need of extra attention from the teacher. But this is not so. Class size is not smaller in lower-income areas; in fact it is somewhat larger. By income halves the distribution is:

INCOME	CLASS SIZE
A (below $7000)	30.6
B (above $7000)	28.8

Thus, on the average, there are almost two extra students in each class in lower-income schools. The distribution by major income groups is as follows.

INCOME GROUP	CLASS SIZE
I ($3000—)	29.7
II ($5000—)	30.9
III ($7000—)	28.6
IV ($9000—)	29.5

The heavier class load in lower-income schools is quite the reverse of what would be expected, considering the low achievement scores and high delinquency rates in these schools. (Class size is actually much larger at all income levels than the tables indicate, since the board of education includes all staff members, not just teachers, in its computation of class size.)

Transported Pupils and Overcrowding

For some strange but possibly significant reason, there has always been much discussion and protest about over-crowded conditions in the high schools of Big City, while at the same time little has been said about overcrowding at the elementary-school level. Perhaps this results from the fact that overcrowding at the high-school level occurs mostly in upper-income areas, while overcrowding in the elementary schools is more common in lower-income schools.

Not long ago in Big City a number of elementary schools were operating on half-day sessions because of overcrowding. Recently these half-day sessions were discontinued, and children from crowded schools are now being transported by bus to less crowded schools. This seems to be a better solution to the problem than half-day sessions, but it is still far from satisfactory.

Transporting children out of their own area to schools which are often miles away involves extra time and special problems for the child. It takes him away from many of his neighborhood friends and throws him into association with children he will not play with after school. It complicates matters for parents, making it difficult and often impossible for them to take part in school activities, visit the school, join parent organizations, or talk to teachers about their children's progress. The distance also makes it difficult for the child to return for after-school classes and programs. In short, it is far from being a good solution to the problem of overcrowding. Yet, probably because lower-income groups do not exert much pressure on the schools, very little is said in protest about the situation.

An investigation of these transported pupils in Big City shows that 3.4 per cent of all elementary-school children in the lowest-income half (below $7000) are transported each day to schools out of their neighborhood, while only half as many, 1.7 per cent, in the upper-income half are transported to other schools.

Teachers

Qualified and competent teachers are indispensable to good education; yet, as in most occupations, it is often difficult to distinguish the competent from the incompetent.

Standards which must be met by individuals seeking to qualify as teachers vary from community to community and state to state. In Big City, as in most other large urban communities, the applicant for a permanent position is required to have a bachelor's degree, practice teaching experience, the required number of hours in education courses, and the state teaching certificate that shows these requirements have been met.

There can be no doubt that teaching standards are subject to much legitimate criticism, that many who qualify under the rules turn out to be poor teachers, while others who would make excellent teachers are sometimes denied teaching certificates for trivial reasons.

Nevertheless, some standards of competence must be established and enforced, as they are in all other professions and skilled jobs. Many persons who earn a Ph.D. do so only because they are insistent drones willing to spend the required number of years—more, if necessary—accumulating and footnoting meaningless and unrelated bits of information. Still, colleges and universities generally require that regular faculty members, however brilliant they may be, shall have earned a Ph.D. before they are granted status and tenure.

Periodically members of the medical profession are exposed as incompetent even though they have been able to meet the standards set for acceptance into the profession. Yet the degree standards of the medical profession are seldom challenged, and the *right* of the profession to establish standards seems never to be questioned.

Into the ranks of every profession persons have been admitted who are in fact unqualified, though they have been able to meet the formal admission requirements. At the same time there are always those who are barred from formal acceptance despite demonstrated excellence. Men have been jailed for "illegal practice of medicine," though they have performed, while working under the eyes of skilled practitioners, hundreds of apparently successful surgical operations—without ever having earned a diploma from an accredited medical school.

Professions, being by nature bureaucratic, must establish rules of thumb by which the "qualified" may be selected from among the applicants. While the "qualified" teacher is not necessarily competent, neither is the "qualified" attorney, physician, or engineer. It must be assumed, however, that the qualified person is more likely to be competent than those who have not met the formal standards and who lack the required college training or successful teaching experience.

Most of the "unqualified" teachers in Big City are classified as ESRPs—that is, they teach but possess only the status of Emergency Substitute in a Regular Position. These ESRPs make up a large part of the teaching staff in some areas and, as might be expected, they are heavily concentrated in lower-income schools. A few ESRPs *are* qualified teachers with regular teaching certificates who, for one reason or another, work as substitute teachers.

Some of them are women with families who would rather not be bound by a contract but prefer the freedom of substitute status.

It is not known, however, how many of these substitutes *are* fully qualified teachers. Records of this sort are not kept, or at least were not available for study. Nor were statistics on the exact qualifications of these permanent substitutes known or available.

It is strange, in a sense, that such records are not kept, since so many apparently irrelevant and rather trivial statistics are recorded by the board of education. Data on the qualifications of teachers could certainly be classed as "vital statistics," yet such records are apparently ignored, along with other important data about the age, experience, and educational background of teachers. Informal reports are, however, that few of these permanent substitutes are qualified teachers with regular certificates.

Undoubtedly there should be room in the schools for competent people who do not have all the teaching prerequisites. Just as certainly such teachers should not be assigned in unbalanced proportions to lower-income areas.

Yet in Big City ESRPs are distributed among the various income levels as follows.

	INCOME LEVEL	ESRPS (PERCENTAGE OF TOTAL TEACHING TIME)
1	$3000—	5.2%
2		12.0
3		17.8
4		11.3
5		16.8
6	$5000—	24.0
7		15.7

INCOME LEVEL		ESRPS (PERCENTAGE OF TOTAL TEACHING TIME)
8		24.4
9		10.8
10		17.7
11		22.5
12		7.4
13		19.0
14		22.7
15		14.0
16	$7000—	7.5
17		6.0
18		8.2
19		.8
20		2.2
21		5.1
22		0
23		6.8
24	$9000—	3.9
25		9.6
26		6.1

In some lower-income groups the teaching time of ESRPs constitutes almost 25 per cent of total teaching time. In effect this means that about one out of every four teachers in these groups is unqualified, according to the certification rules.

A sharp contrast is apparent between groups in the lower- and the upper-income halves. Only two groups in the lower-income half (under $7000) are under 10.0 per cent, while all groups in the upper half are under the 10.0 per cent level.

The percentage of ESRPs in group 1, and in all groups under $5000, is unexpectedly low. The tendency to give slightly better services to the lowest income group, as compared with the second-lowest group, is noted in several other instances too. The explanation for this is not known; perhaps it is only when students are extremely destitute that their needs are obvious enough to attract some small amount of attention.

The distribution of ESRPs by major income groups and income halves is as follows.

INCOME GROUP	ESRPS
I ($3000—)	13.9%
II ($5000—)	19.1
III ($7000—)	5.4
IV ($9000—)	4.5
A (below $7000)	17.9%
B (above $7000)	5.5

The heaviest concentration of ESRPs is found in group II, where they teach almost one out of every five teaching hours.

In the income halves the per cent of ESRPs in group A is more than three times greater than in group B.

The heavy loading of ESRPs in lower-income groups indicates that children in these groups have what must be termed "inferior" teachers. It also indicates that the schools are spending considerably less on teachers' salaries in lower-income schools, since ESRPs are paid much less than regular teachers and receive virtually none of the regular teacher's fringe benefits.

More money is spent on teachers' salaries in upper-income schools for another reason: teachers in upper-income schools tend to be more experienced and consequently higher up in the salary schedule, because of annual increments, than the inexperienced teachers in lower-income schools.

Teachers in higher-income schools tend to be more experienced because teachers with seniority prefer to teach in them, and seniority usually counts when teaching assignments are made. Since experienced teachers often choose to teach in upper-income schools, the new and inexperienced teachers are given the "left-over" assignments in lower-income schools. In Big City a beginning teacher with a bachelor's degree earns $4700 a year; an experienced teacher at the top of the scale earns $7400 a year. Thus $2700 more is being spent on the experienced teacher, who, more often than not, is working in an upper-income school.

Recently school administrators have tried to attract more teachers to the city by placing new teachers in "better" schools in upper-income areas, but these efforts met with serious resistance from high-seniority teachers who wanted to teach in the "better" schools themselves. So, despite efforts to change placement practices, it is still generally true that inexperienced teachers (as well as unqualified teachers) tend to be concentrated in lower-income schools. No information was available from the board of education about the precise distribution of these inexperienced teachers.

There are those who claim that inexperienced teachers are just as good as, if not better than, experienced teachers; their youth and their interest and enthusiasm, they say, make up for their lack of experience. It is rather strange that claims of this sort are made about teachers but not about other occupational groups. The same people who deprecate experience in teachers want doctors, lawyers, machinists, stenographers, etc., to be completely experienced in their work. For some reason they assume that teachers are different, that they, alone among all occupational groups, cannot profit very much from experience.

It seems likely that, other things being equal, an experienced teacher is much to be preferred to an inexperienced teacher. Teachers themselves, experienced as well as inexperienced, will be the first to admit this. No doubt many teachers do not grow old gracefully. Some become harsh and unbending with the passing years, resisting new ideas and all suggestions of change; still, a teacher can become expert at her job only through experience, and expertness is as necessary in teaching as in any other occupation.

Yet a large proportion of inexperienced teachers in lower-income schools would probably be acceptable if extra staff were added to compensate for this inexperience and for the much larger sums of money being spent on teaching staff in upper-income schools. Perhaps this type of adjustment is to be preferred to a redistribution of teachers. Certainly as much money should be spent on teachers in poorer areas of the city as is now being spent in wealthier areas.

School Buildings and Facilities

Perhaps the most important and most costly elements of good education, aside from teachers, are school buildings and school facilities. There is no denying that it is *possible* to learn in a one-room school that is run down and lacking in even the barest facilities; just so, it is *possible* to cook in a one-room apartment with only a hot plate or a wood stove and no cooking utensils. But the quality of cooking, for most of those who tried to do it, would in all probability be greatly inferior to what they could turn out in a modern kitchen. Moreover the effort would be tiresome, perhaps exhausting, and needlessly time-consuming. Similarly, in an inadequate school building with substandard facilities, the quality of education in all probability will be inferior, and learning more difficult and certainly less pleasant.

Obviously there is some top limit on the number or quality of facilities required for the best possible education; six stoves in the average kitchen would be no better than one, and indeed might tend to reduce efficiency. But we have not yet reached the point where we need worry about school buildings and facilities being anything more than adequate, at least judging by schools in Big City.

What social class differences are there in school buildings and facilities in the city's elementary schools? The clear answer is that school buildings, and the facilities they contain, are *much less adequate* in lower-income than in upper-income areas. One reason for this is that the schools in lower-income areas are much older than those in higher-income areas, and therefore generally inferior. In the lower-income half (below $7000) 30.5 per cent of all children—almost one out of every three—go to schools that are fifty years old or older. By contrast, no students in the upper-income half attend schools of this age.

The average age of school buildings in Big City is as follows.

INCOME GROUP	YEARS
I ($3000—)	45
II ($5000—)	46
III ($7000—)	26
IV ($9000—)	25

Thus school buildings in the lower-income half are almost twice as old as buildings in the upper-income half.

Certainly the age of school buildings is largely, if not wholly, a geographic accident. Buildings, public and private, tend to be older in the central areas of the city where lower income groups live. The schools are in no way responsible for this accident except in so far as they tend to erect new buildings in the overcrowded and richer fringe areas of the city rather than in the overcrowded central areas of the city.

In Big City at the time of this study, elementary schools in the lower-income areas of the city were both considerably older and considerably more overcrowded than schools in upper-income areas.

The schools, though not responsible for the city's geography and for housing patterns, would seem to bear responsibility for providing compensatory services to students attending school in substandard buildings. Such compensation might be in the form of extra staff or services, or, where advisable, the buildings themselves might be replaced or renovated.

Largely because of age differences, school facilities in upper-income areas of Big City are considerably superior to those in lower-income areas. Table 8 shows the percentage of schools in each income group with either no facilities or with "substandard" facilities of the type indicated.

TABLE 8. Percentage of Schools with No Facilities or Substandard Facilities

| | MAJOR INCOME GROUPS | | | | INCOME HALVES | |
FACILITIES	GROUP I $3000—	GROUP II $5000—	GROUP III $7000—	GROUP IV $9000—	A BELOW $7000	B ABOVE $7000
Science	50%	46%	3%	0%	47%	2%
Conservatory	67	50	6	6	54	6
Art room	11	11	4	0	11	4
Library	11	16	15	11	15	14
Instrumental Music & Speech	78	95	59	39	91	56
Speech	83	88	84	89	86	85
Store Room	6	18	6	6	15	6
Men's & Women's Rest Rooms	61	68	40	16	66	30
Auditorium	5	16	2	6	14	3
Auditorium Activities Room (backstage)	78	95	52	39	91	50
Office	0	11	2	0	8	2
Clinic	17	21	11	11	20	11
Kitchen	44	55	31	17	53	28
Air Raid Shelter	67	61	25	6	62	21

Except for library and speech, all facilities listed are much more adequate in upper-income schools. Perhaps the most unfortunate deficiency is found in science facilities. In the lower-income half, 47 per cent of all schools do not have proper facilities for scientific studies while only 2 per cent of schools in the upper-income half have inadequate facilities.

In some respects school facilities in group II are more deficient than in group I. This is probably attributable to the fact that slum clearance has replaced some of the oldest buildings in low-income areas with new ones.

Big City schools have recently undergone the most thorough examination in their history; consequently, more information about buildings and facilities was available for this study than for any previous study of city schools. The examination was made by a committee of citizens who visited all schools in the city during the course of a year and rated all elements of the school plant. The reports of this committee were issued in a series of weighty volumes which, for our purposes, have been reduced and rearranged to fit the income categories of this study.

Ratings were made by the committee on the basis of ten principal criteria: adequacy, suitability, safety, healthfulness, accessibility, flexibility, efficiency, economy, expansibility, and appearance. The total building scores in Table 9 are the sum of ratings in these ten separate areas. Since a perfect score in each of the ten areas is 100, a perfect total building score would be 1000. (Scores which are *over* 700 are marked with a plus sign, and scores which are *under* 600 are marked with a minus sign.)

TABLE 9. Total Building Scores
(perfect score: 1000)

MINOR INCOME GROUP	SCORES
1	460.6—
2	623.2
3	495.6—
4	580.0—
5	612.7
6	539.3—
7	506.5—
8	583.6—
9	662.3
10	499.9—
11	554.5—

MINOR INCOME GROUP	SCORES
12	566.0—
13	568.8—
14	637.9
15	678.6
16	+733.0
17	673.4
18	+802.1
19	+701.5
20	+754.3
21	+705.8
22	661.0
23	+819.5
24	+798.6
25	+751.0
26	691.7

It will be noted that there are no scores over 700 in the lower-income half (groups 16–26); at the same time there are three groups with scores below 500.

In the upper-income half, eight groups (all but three) have scores over 700, and two groups have scores over 800.

The total building scores by major income groups and income halves follow.

INCOME GROUP	TOTAL BUILDING SCORE
I ($3000—)	573.5
II ($5000—)	578.3
III ($7000—)	688.3
IV ($9000—)	799.3
A (below $7000)	577.0
B (above $7000)	704.9

It will be noted here that, while there is little difference between scores in groups I and II, there is an increase of over 100 points in group III, and an additional increase of over 100 points in group IV.

According to the citizens' committee rating chart, adequacy refers to the relationship between the size of the site and building space on the one hand, and the number of students to be served on the other. Included in this rating are such items as the adequacy of the school site, parking space, classroom and laboratory facilities, classrooms, storage space, and space for administrative staff. Major group ratings follow (100 is a perfect score).

INCOME GROUP	ADEQUACY
I	49.5
II	48.2
III	63.5
IV	65.5
A	48.5
B	63.8

In the minor groups, the lowest score was found in group 3—36.2; the highest score went to group 25—68.0, with a difference between the two groups of 31.8 points.

The suitability rating includes "those features, such as type of plant and the facilities available, which enable the school to house satisfactorily the particular educational program to be carried on." In other words this rating refers to how suitable the plant and facilities are, considering the needs of the school program.

Among the questions raised in this rating were: Are the site, playground areas, and soil properly developed? Are classrooms suitably equipped for small group work? Are there suitable classroom facilities, audio-visual materials, bulletin boards, and other classroom equipment? Major group ratings follow.

INCOME GROUP	SUITABILITY
I	45.1
II	42.2
III	57.2
IV	59.5
A	43.0
B	57.7

Safety refers to those features of the school plant which make the building structurally sound and protect the students from hazards of traffic, fire, and accidents. Major group ratings in safety follow.

INCOME GROUP	SAFETY
I	71.0
II	68.0
III	83.0
IV	85.3
A	69.0
B	83.6

According to these ratings, upper-income schools are considerably safer than lower-income schools.

The healthfulness rating refers to the "degree to which pupils are insured freedom from dirt and excessive noise, and provided with satisfactory facilities for lighting, heating, ventilation, and sanitation, and a plentiful and convenient supply of pure water. In general, the features of

the building designed to protect and promote the good
health of the pupils are covered in this category."

INCOME GROUP	HEALTHFULNESS
I	63.8
II	65.9
III	81.0
IV	79.4
A	65.3
B	80.7

"Appearance" refers to "how the school looks and
whether it is pleasing to the eye. Attention is directed to
landscaping, color harmony, appropriateness of furnish-
ing, and use of decoration."

INCOME GROUP	APPEARANCE
I	65.9
II	74.9
III	85.9
IV	90.0
A	72.6
B	86.7

From these various ratings it appears that upper-income
schools are more attractive, healthful, safer, more suitable,
and more adequate than lower-income schools.

What do these building scores mean to students in their
daily school life? How does "healthfulness," for example,
affect what happens to them during the course of a day's
school work?

The scores in Table 10 answer these questions perhaps

better than the scores in the ten principal categories; these scores are derived from but are more detailed and meaningful than the ten categories:

TABLE 10. Building Scores (numbers in parentheses indicate "perfect" scores)

	GROUP A (UNDER $7000)	GROUP B (OVER $7000)
Adequacy		
Size of site (20)	4.6	9.6
Size of parking (3)	.9	1.3
Adequate play areas (15)	2.4	3.6
Size of classrooms (10)	5.5	6.1
Equipment classrooms (5)	3.8	3.9
Enough classrooms (15)	7.2	10.3
Enough bulletin boards (2)	1.0	1.5
Enough staff, administrative space, & equipment (5)	2.2	2.9
Suitability		
Shop work equipment (5)	1.7	2.4
Homemaking equipment (5)	1.3	2.6
Art facilities (5)	2.8	3.8
Music (storage, seating, practice rooms) (5)	1.9	2.8
Assembly & public performances (2)	.8	1.2
Hot lunches—suitable provisions (3)	.7	1.8
Lockers & wardrobes (2)	1.1	1.4
Science equipment (5)	1.7	3.0
Community facilities (3)	1.1	2.0
Size of building & equipment (5)	3.2	4.2
Library facilities (5)	1.9	2.5
Health & physical education (5)	2.0	2.9
Safety		
Approaches free of hazards (heavy traffic) (5)	2.2	3.2
Site hazards (5)	4.1	4.8
Playground hazards (5)	3.5	3.8
Hazards walks & drives (5)	2.6	2.8
Fire-control facilities (5)	3.7	4.4

TABLE 10. Building Scores (numbers in parentheses indicate
"perfect" scores) (continued)

	GROUP A (UNDER $7000)	GROUP B (OVER $7000)
Structural hazards in the building (5)	2.9	4.6
Stairway safe (5)	3.4	4.6
Non-skid floors (3)	2.1	2.6
Corridor hazards (3)	1.1	2.2
Fire hazards (10)	5.8	8.9
Healthfulness		
Heating & ventilation satisfactory (10)	7.0	7.9
Drinking fountains in corridors (5)	2.9	3.7
Toilet facilities (adequate & suitable) (10)	5.2	8.5
Playground drinking fountains (5)	.2	.7
Proper lighting—all rooms (15)	9.6	10.5
Seats proper size (15)	8.2	7.7
Atmosphere in the area (10)	6.0	9.4
Saloons in area (10)	6.2	9.2
Appearance		
Site environment attractive (5)	2.3	4.6
Site attractive—planned & landscaped (15)	8.8	12.7
Building attractive (5)	2.8	4.2
Building in good repair (10)	8.0	9.2
Site well kept (10)	7.5	8.5
Pupil rooms cheerful (20)	14.3	16.3

A typical upper-income child, then, goes to a school that
is safer, more suitable and adequate for his needs, more
attractive inside and out, with much better facilities in
most subjects, including science, music, art and library,
and also with better lighting, lavatory, and other health
facilities than the school attended by the average lower-
income child.

Table 11 summarizes the most important deficiencies of
elementary-school buildings according to citizens' committee ratings.

It should be noted that, in this tabulation, group A (the lower-income half) consists of 104 schools, group B of 108 schools. The two groups therefore are close enough in size to permit a comparison of this kind.

TABLE 11. Number of Schools with Serious Building Deficiencies

	GROUP A (BELOW $7000)	GROUP B (ABOVE $7000)
Classrooms entirely too small	16	8
Totally inadequate labs & special rooms (size)	15	9
Inadequate labs & special rooms (size)	15	4
Totally inadequate lab & special room *equipment*	25	12
Totally unsuitable space for shop work	54	33
Totally unsuitable art facilities	17	7
Dangerous traffic hazards at pupil approaches to school	25	7
Located in industrially hazardous area	8	0
Need safety fence	10	4
Very dangerous playground hazards	7	5
Totally inadequate provisions for science instruction	41	9
Totally inadequate classroom water supply	29	9
Building combustible	34	3
Music room & facilities totally inadequate	24	14

In the lower-income half, twelve buildings received "lowest" ratings (indicating that they are not fit for use), while in the upper-income half there were no such buildings.

Of buildings with "best" ratings, three were in the lower half and eight were in the upper-income half.

The percentage of schools receiving "low" ratings—"poor" and "fair"—follows.

INCOME GROUP	POOR	TOTAL: POOR & FAIR
I ($3000—)	19.5%	54.9%
II ($5000—)	19.6	49.5
III ($7000—)	1.2	14.5
IV ($9000—)	0	5.3

These ratings leave no doubt about the substantial superiority of school buildings and school facilities in upper-income areas. In sharp contrast to the ratings of upper-income schools, almost 20 per cent of school buildings in groups I and II had "poor" ratings, and almost 50 per cent had either "poor" or "fair" ratings.

Free Meals or Milk

What may be the most flagrant example of unequally distributed school services in Big City is to be found in the free-lunch program.

Most schools in Big City have cafeterias where students may buy hot lunches or where they will be served free lunches if they can "prove beyond doubt" that they are unable to pay. A very sizable percentage of the city's schools, however, do not have lunchrooms and do not serve meals at all, free or otherwise.

The following table shows the percentage of schools in each income group which, according to board of education data, serve *no* free meals or free milk.

INCOME GROUP	PERCENTAGE OF SCHOOLS SERVING NO FREE MEALS OR MILK
I ($3000—)	42%
II ($5000—)	22
III ($7000—)	11
IV ($9000—)	22

So it is that in the lowest-income group, among children who are likely to be in greatest need of balanced, wholesome meals at lunchtime and who are most likely to be undernourished and ailing, almost half (42 per cent) go to schools where free meals and free milk are not available. Meals, it is claimed, cannot be served in these schools because cafeteria facilities are not present. This is a questionable excuse, however, since it is possible for schools to serve cold lunches (sandwiches, fruit, salads, milk, etc.) in the absence of cooking facilities. Perhaps the "reason" rather than the "excuse" for this failure to provide free lunches for needy children is the lack of administrative interest in the program. Several years ago, in fact, an attempt was made to eliminate the program completely, the contention being that welfare agencies and not the schools should feed hungry children, but the move was so hotly contested in the community by those who feared it would result in no program at all that the effort was abandoned.

In addition to being denied *free* lunches where need is obvious, children attending schools without lunchrooms are also denied the subsidies that are being put into the *paid* lunch program. Children in upper-income schools, where hot lunches are usually provided, can buy lunches as cheaply as they can be made for them at home. In addition, these children are being fed wholesome, balanced meals; they are saved the time and inconvenience of going home for lunch, and their families are saved the effort of preparing lunch for them.

In low-income areas, where mothers often work and are not home at lunchtime, children may not eat "lunch" at all. Snacks, candy bars, Cokes are consumed instead.

Often, out of poverty, neglect, and ignorance of what constitutes a balanced meal, the same fare is consumed at other meals as well.

Providing wholesome free meals for *all* low-income children would no doubt greatly improve their health, strength and vitality, at the same time increasing their capacity and willingness to learn. Out of gratitude for such a program, these deprived children might develop some basis for loyalty and attachment to the schools.

In order to reduce truancy and delinquency in "difficult" schools in other areas and other countries, it is customary to furnish all students with free meals, with no affidavits of poverty required. In the New York "600" schools, the system seems to be getting some results. In Sweden, where free lunches are served to *all* school children, the health and vitality of the nation's school population are reported to have been very favorably affected by the added nourishment.

In Big City perhaps all that could be expected from any immediate program would be that all children with obvious nutritional needs be furnished free lunches in school.

3

Life at Home

Yea, a man may say, Thou hast faith and I have works:
show me thy faith without thy works and I will show thee
my faith by my works. . . .
But wilt thou know, O vain man, that faith without works
is dead? Seest thou how faith wrought with his works, and
by works was faith made perfect?
                    —General Epistle of James 2:18, 20, 22

LIFE AT HOME

School occupies only part of the child's day. The rest of the day is spent at home—as are weekends, holidays, summer vacations, and the formative pre-school years. Because of the time spent and the learning that takes place, what happens to the child at home and in his neighborhood usually has a greater influence on him than what happens in school. Indeed, what happens to him at home, and the social class conditioning he gets there, will largely determine what happens to him in school. The child is "made" at home, and he is accepted, rejected, or ignored by the school according to how well this homemade product meets the tolerance standards set up by the school, standards which are mainly based on class factors.

An examination of the out-of-school life of children in

139

Big City gives us some insight into the operation of these class factors and their carry-over into the life of the school.

The figures in Table 12 are based on 1950 Census data; they are somewhat dated but the fact that the relative standing of the major income groups, as measured by *revised* Census data, is still much the same seems to justify their use. The figures are based on ratings made by the board of education, and they indicate the percentage of schools with "highest" ratings (top 20 per cent) in each category.

TABLE 12. Percentage of Schools with "Highest" Ratings—Top 20 per cent

	GROUP I ($3000—)	GROUP II ($5000—)	GROUP III ($7000—)	GROUP IV ($9000)
1. Number of laborers	92%	12%	0	0
2. Persons with some college training	0	8	14%	100%
3. Homes needing repair	75	14	0	0
4. Value of owner-occupied single homes	0	2	34	83
5. Population density per square mile	84	10	0	0
6. General Public Assistance	83	15	1	0
7. Deaths from tuberculosis	79	8	0	0
8. Truancy, children 5–19	42	17	1	0
9. Truancy, court cases	50	13	1	0

Not surprisingly these ratings show that homes in lower-income areas are in worse condition than those in upper-income areas, housing is more overcrowded, truancy, tuberculosis, and public assistance rates are higher, and there are more laborers and fewer people with some college training. These are just a few of the environmental handicaps which make it difficult for lower-income children to run a fair race with upper-income children in school. The list could continue at some length.

Community Problems

A research agency in Big City has computed the relationship between family income and various community factors. This relationship is shown statistically in terms of "coefficients of rank correlation."

The closest correlation between two items is represented by the number 1.00. The closer the number is to 1.00, the higher the correlation, and the closer is the relationship between the two factors being compared. A correlation of .90, for example, indicates that the factors in question are very closely related.

A minus sign in front of a number in the rather complicated-looking Table 13 indicates that the two factors are *inversely* related. For example, the minus sign in front of the first number in the table (—.83) indicates that in areas where old-age assistance rates are *high,* income tends to be *low.* To put it another and slightly different way, people receiving old-age assistance are likely to have low incomes and to live in low-income areas.

Almost all these community factors are quite closely related to family income, some more than others. Interestingly enough, "Offenses known to police" is not so closely related to low income as "Juvenile court cases." This might indicate that lower-income youths are more likely to be brought to court for offenses known to police than are upper-income youths. Also, the low correlation of "Offenses known to police" and family income (—.66) indicates that offenses are committed by upper-income youths

TABLE 13. Community Problems (Coefficients of Rank Correlation) by Sub-Communities

COMMUNITY FACTORS	CORRELATION WITH AVERAGE FAMILY INCOME
Public Assistance	
Old-age assistance	—.83
Aid to dependent children	—.90
General public assistance	—.94
Unemployed persons	—.70
Behavior	
Neglected children	—.84
Truancy	—.87
Violations juvenile code	—.85
Juvenile court cases	—.90
Composite delinquency index	—.93
Offenses against person	—.92
Offenses against property	—.57
Offenses known to police	—.66
Vital Data	
Total deaths (crude rate)	—.72
Total deaths (age adjusted rate)	—.87
Tuberculosis deaths	—.91
Infant deaths	—.53
Illegitimate births	—.87
Occupation	
Professional & managerial workers	.73
Laborers & service workers	—.92
Housing	
Average monthly rent	.69
Average value homes	.81
Homes—poor condition	—.94
Overcrowding	—.89
Population density	—.92
Socio-economic classification of community areas	.94

with greater frequency than might be assumed, judging by
Detention School admissions. Perhaps many of the offenses committed by upper-income youths are not serious
enough for arrest or conviction, or perhaps offenses committed by these youths are simply overlooked and easily
forgiven by the police. Only further investigation can
provide a reliable explanation.

The low correlation between "Average monthly rent"
and family income (.69) indicates that rents in low-income
areas tend to be quite high in proportion to income, and
that low-income families are paying rather dearly for the
privilege of living in slum housing.

Parks and Recreation Areas

There are more parks and recreation areas in the upper-
income areas of Big City than in the lower-income areas.
In two large sections of the highest-income area there are
30 acres of public recreation area for every 10,000 people,
the highest rate in the city. The lowest rate is found in the
oldest part of the city, near the downtown area where the
lowest-income groups live. In one large section of this
area (130,000 population) there are only 2.6 acres of
recreation area per 10,000 people—as compared with 30
acres in the highest-income area.

Thus, the people with the greatest need for recreation
areas are being provided with the fewest facilities. As we
have seen, low-income groups tend to have high delinquency, disease, and mortality rates. Expanded play
areas, one might hope, would reduce the incidence of
these and other pressing problems in low-income areas.

Children in these areas also tend to be much less mobile than children in upper-income areas. Poorer children (because their parents usually do not have cars or the money for travel or summer camps or even for local bus transportation) are virtually imprisoned in the crowded areas where they live. When recreation facilities in these areas are not adequate, it is very difficult for lower-income children to go elsewhere to find them. As a result, they are forced to remain in these crowded areas, with few recreational outlets and nothing to do—except get into trouble. The trouble that begins on a street corner may not end when the school bell rings.

Experiences of Children

We have seen that lower-income children live in run-down, overcrowded homes and in neighborhoods with high death, crime, and disease rates and limited recreational facilities.

Related to these deficiences, and also significant in school success or failure, is the fact that most lower-income children are deprived of the broad range of life experiences open to upper-income children. The lower-income child, in fact, seldom emerges from his neighborhood confinement in order to test the experiences of the outside world. He is restricted to his own back yard and its immediate area for at least several reasons, among which are: he is afraid to go out of his neighborhood; the outside world is afraid to let him come out; he does not have the money or the opportunity to go out; he does not know enough about the outside world to know where to go.

Whatever the causes, the limited view of the world that

results makes school work more difficult for the lower-income child. He is denied the life experiences which give children confidence in themselves and interest in their studies. Such experiences greatly increase reading potential by providing some familiarity with the vocabulary and subject matter of books. In addition they offer a better basis for understanding and evaluating all the subject matter that must be learned in school.

It is axiomatic in education that "we learn best what we learn from experience"; it is also a simple and accepted educational axiom that "travel broadens one," even if travel means only a trip to the local zoo, museum, or department store for the school child. Yet the low-income child is often denied these experiences, according to Judith I. Krugman, who studied a group of underprivileged children.

Most of these children have missed many out-of-school experiences which children in middle-class homes have had from an early age—experiences which develop concepts, abilities, and attitudes favorable to school success. Many of the parents cannot supply these experiences because they are limited by their own problems, by lack of time and energy after work, as well as by different values and often by ignorance of appropriate children's experiences.

And so the school is faced with these gaps in the children's backgrounds. If it knows what these lacks are, it can help to compensate for them to some degree. Outside of school, very few of the children in the experimental class in the third grade had been read to, had children's books at home, had creative playthings like blocks or paints, had been taken to local places of interest like zoos or museums. Some had never had a birthday party and very few knew their birthdays.

The majority had more limited vocabularies than children of equivalent ability from more privileged homes.[1]

In contrast, children from upper-income families usually have rich life experiences. One teacher in an upper-income school says of her students: "In a neighborhood like this there's something about the children, you just feel like you're accomplishing so much more. They go places and see things, and they know what you're talking about. For instance, you might be teaching social studies or geography. . . . You bring something up and a child says, 'Oh, my parents took me to see that in the museum.' You can just do more with material like that."

E. Volberding concludes from a study of eleven-year-olds: "Middle-class and the upper-lower-class children were far more active and adventurous in their out-of-school living than were the lower-lower-class children. The hypothesis has been advanced that the lower-lower-class child is inhibited because of insecurity which arises from the lack of status of his family group in the community and the lack of social contacts of his parents. These lacks affect the child's social experience and his confidence." [2]

To provide anything approximating equal educational opportunity, the schools must try to open up this world of experience to lower-income children—through trips, television, movies, and other media. Trips may be especially valuable, since they will familiarize children with commonplace things in their own localities, thereby pushing back the walls of their neighborhood confinement. Trips may also be a source of considerable interest and personal satisfaction to these children, as well as intellectual stimulation.

In Big City schools lower-income children seldom go on anything but short-distance walking trips. School buses are rarely, if ever, available and regular bus fare is out of the question. Moreover, since lower-income parents usually lack either cars or daytime leisure, they cannot provide transportation for their children, as upper-income parents occasionally do; consequently, lower-income children, according to reports, do not go on as many "field trips" in school as upper-income children.

Lower-income children are also much less likely than upper-income children to belong to organizations. In one recent year in Big City, 37 per cent of working-class boys of age fourteen to sixteen, and only 17 per cent of upper-middle-class boys, belonged to no organizations at all. This means that more than twice as many working-class boys were non-joiners without any organizational ties. More than half of the upper-middle-class boys (52 per cent) belonged to more than one organization, as compared with 31 per cent of working-class boys.

An older report (1949) shows that Boy or Girl Scout memberships in Big City were as follows.

upper middle class	46%
lower middle class	22
upper lower class	23
lower lower class	15

Thus Scout membership rates were more than three times as high in the upper middle as in the lower lower class.

Joining constructive group activities could give lower-income youths some of the confidence and social poise that they seem to lack, but here again they tend to be denied these experiences in almost inverse proportion to need.

4

Senior High Schools

And other sheep I have, which are not of this fold:
them also I must bring and they shall hear my voice;
and there shall be one fold and one shepherd.

—John 10:16

SENIOR HIGH SCHOOLS

Hᴵɢʜ ꜱᴄʜᴏᴏʟꜱ in Big City are much like elementary schools in their social class characteristics. The differences among schools, however, are sometimes less clearly defined than in the smaller and more homogeneous elementary schools. High schools are large institutions drawing students from a wide geographic area, some from very low and some from very high income pockets. Because of this, differences among high schools tend to be rather muted in some cases.

Nevertheless, social class is very apparent at the high-school level in a number of significant ways. Social class distinctions are also present *within* each high school, much more than within each elementary school, though it was not our purpose to explore these distinctions, interesting as they may be.

In some ways high schools reveal the operation of the social class system better than elementary schools do. In Big City all elementary-school children, regardless of origins or aspirations, study much the same subjects and proceed through the same curriculum. It is only at the high-school level that they begin to go their separate ways. In the high schools students are very methodically sorted out into various categories—like mail in a post office—depending on the school's appraisal of their destination in life.

In elementary schools students are often separated into "ability" groups, usually of a rather temporary nature. At the high-school level this "ability" grouping system usually becomes greatly exaggerated and more permanent and inflexible in character.

Some high schools in Big City sort students into "ability" groups (on the basis of IQ tests) which are so rigidly segregated that students in one group have little or no contact with students in other groups. Some schools, avoiding this kind of semi-caste system, sort their students into subtler types of "ability" groups.

In addition to "ability" separations, all high schools in Big City sort students into three basic curriculums, chiefly on the basis of presumed "ability"; these curriculums are: college preparatory, vocational (and commercial), and general (the catch-all category). Placement in these curriculums may determine the student's entire future life. If a student is placed, for example, in a general or vocational curriculum (at ages ranging from twelve to fourteen), he will have great difficulty qualifying for college entry or remaining in college should he be admitted. His chances, therefore, of moving into professional or highly skilled jobs will be similarly limited.

In principle, of course, and on paper, the child and the parent have the final say about curriculum selection. In actual practice, however, the school often makes the decision. Students who are not thought qualified for college prep are persuaded to take other courses, or they are simply not admitted. Students regarded as qualified for college prep are persuaded to enter. The school's guiding hand is often firm and directive. The lower-income parent, knowing little about school affairs or vocational preparation, is usually willing to follow the school's lead.

Another basic element in this sorting process is the high-school drop-out. About 50 per cent of all students in the city drop out of school before completing the twelfth grade. Without a high-school diploma, these students are virtually frozen into the occupational and status positions of their parents and their social class. As we shall see, the heaviest concentration of drop-outs is in the lowest-income groups.

Still another aspect of the sorting and selecting process is the social system of the high school and the student's increasing awareness of his status and social position in relation to other students. Albert Hieronymus says that "in elementary grades there appears to be little grouping along class lines, while in high school 70 to 75 per cent of students' 'best friends' come from their own social class." The high-school student's sudden awareness of his position, and his acceptance or rejection of it, seem to have a marked influence on his attitudes and on his school activities.

There are only seventeen high schools in Big City, excluding schools which are wholly or largely vocational.
The family income levels in these seventeen schools, according to revised Census data, are the following.

SCHOOL	INCOME IN SCHOOL AREA
1	$5043
2	5315
3	5452
4	5643
5	5700
6	6260
7	6600
8	6893
9	7220
10	7324
11	7486
12	7685
13	8000
14	8114
15	8430
16	8724
17	9503

Because there are so few schools, major income group
divisions have been made at every one thousand dollars of
income instead of every two thousand, as in the elementary
schools. As a result there are five major income groups
instead of the four which were used in the discussion of
elementary schools.

Achievement Tests

Standardized achievement tests had not been given in Big City high schools at the time of this study. It has been only recently, in fact, that, under the direction of a new superintendent, tests were given in the city's elementary schools. The reasons for the failure of previous administrations to give achievement tests are rather obscure. Certainly there are few things more vital to the successful administration of a school system than information about the achievement levels of students in that system.

Even now nothing is known about the achievement levels of high-school students in the city. The only clues available at the time of this writing were Iowa test scores from small groups of students in some of the city's high schools. Because so few students were tested in this sample run, the results do not have very great significance; but they are interesting. The scores on page 156, for example, come from a typical home-room group in high school 1, the lowest-income school. They are reading scores of twenty-seven 10B students on the Iowa Achievement Test. A 10B student reading at grade level should have had a score of 10.0.

Little wonder, in view of such reading performances as this, that administrators apparently would rather not give standardized achievement tests or expose these scores to public—or even private—view.

The average reading score of this 10B group is 7.4 (seventh grade plus), more than two and a half grades below grade level.

Not one of the students in this group is reading at or

above grade level, although two are very close to grade level.

READING SCORES

9.9
9.7
8.9
8.6
8.5
8.4
8.3
7.9
7.9
7.8
7.7
7.7
7.5
7.3
7.2
7.1
7.1
7.1
7.0
6.9
6.7
6.7
6.4
6.1
6.1
5.2
<u>4.5</u>

Average Score   7.4

One student is reading at fourth-grade level (4.5), or five and a half grades below grade level. One student is reading at fifth-grade level (5.2), or somewhat less than five grades below grade level. Six students are reading at sixth-grade level, or four grades below grade level.

Almost one-third of the students in this 10B group are reading four grades or more below grade level. This is all the more remarkable since, *in this lowest-income high school, a 10B home room is a rather select group, many of the poorest readers having already dropped out of school.*

In and Out of School

Attendance and Work Permits

Attendance was about the same as in the elementary schools, as these figures show.

INCOME GROUP	ATTENDANCE DURING A TYPICAL WEEK
I ($5000—)	90.6%
II ($6000—)	92.7
III ($7000—)	94.3
IV ($8000—)	94.8
V ($9000—)	94.9
A (below $7000)	91.4
B (above $7000)	94.6

In the upper-income half, 3.2 per cent more students attended school than in the lower half. If 3.2 per cent more students in the lower-income half had been in school, it would have amounted to an increase in attendance of almost six hundred students. In the major income groups, the difference between groups I and V is 4.3 per cent.

Jobs: In order to work, an under-age youth must obtain a work permit. The following table shows the distribution of these permits. Figures in the right-hand column are permits issued per hundred students.

INCOME GROUP	PERMITS ISSUED
I	12.3
II	22.9
III	32.5
IV	32.1
V	22.3
A	15.0
B	30.9

A rather unexpected pattern is revealed in these figures. Students in the lowest-income group (group I) are most in need of jobs, yet are least likely to have them.

Of course job opportunities are often very limited for underprivileged youths. They are extremely limited in the case of Negro youths; a recent study of Connecticut schools shows that, while 57 per cent of white girls desiring work found it, only 4 per cent of Negro girls who looked for jobs were able to find them. Negro boys have almost as difficult a time finding work.

The failure of lower-income youths to find jobs, pocket money, and something constructive to do with their leisure is probably a contributing factor to the high delinquency rates found in these groups.

It may also contribute to the lower-income youth's general lack of purpose in school. If he comes to think that he is unemployable, that he hasn't a chance of getting a job—even less a good job—he is not likely to have much enthusiasm for school work (which is, after all, mainly job-preparation).

Pupil Turnover

Again in the high schools, transiency is closely associated with income. The number of students who either left or entered school during the course of one semester was—per 100 students in each income group—as follows. These are transfers, not drop-outs.

INCOME GROUP	TURNOVER
I ($5000—)	48.4
II ($6000—)	38.8
III ($7000—)	30.8
IV ($8000—)	23.9
V ($9000—)	17.7
A (below $7000)	44.8
B (above $7000)	26.3

The lowest-income group, as we see, had a turnover rate in one semester of almost 50 per cent, counting all incoming and outgoing students. This is considerably more than twice the rate of the highest-income group; in fact it is more nearly three times the rate.

Success—Failure

Special Rewards

Ford Employee Scholarships: Each year the Ford Motor Company awards college scholarships to the children of Ford employees. The award is four years of college tuition with up to $720 a year living expenses. The distribution of these scholarships, by income halves, during a one-year period was:

INCOME HALF	NUMBER OF SCHOLARSHIPS
A (below $7000)	1
B (above $7000)	10

The vast majority of Ford employees make less than $7000 a year, yet only one of the eleven scholarships was awarded to a student in the lower-income half.

University Freshman Honors Class: One of the state universities offers a special accelerated program for entering freshmen. Students are selected for this honors program from among the top scholastic 5 per cent of the entering freshman class.

Of the fifteen Big City students selected during one recent semester, only two were from income group A (below $7000). One of these two students was the son of a school principal. The other thirteen students were from the upper-income half.

Of the fifty students selected from the Big City metropolitan area, only these fifteen students were from Big City proper; the others were from suburban areas, indicating that the highest awards may be most heavily concentrated in suburban areas.

Scholastic Awards: Top National Scholastic Awards for writing were given to sixteen Big City students during one recent year. Only one was given to a student in income group A; the other fifteen went to students in the upper-income half.

National Merit Scholarships: One of the most coveted of all academic awards, and one of the most difficult to win since selections are made on the basis of competitive exams, is the National Merit Scholarship.

During one recent semester, the eight winners of these scholarships in Big City all came from the upper-income half (over $7000). No awards were given to students in the lower-income half.

These findings are confirmed by Horace Mann Bond's

study of the number of "workers" in each occupational group required to produce one Merit Scholar; his results are shown in Table 14.[1]

TABLE 14. Workers Required to Produce
Merit Scholars

MAJOR U.S. CENSUS OCCUPATIONAL GROUPS, RANKED IN ORDER OF PRODUCTIVITY OF MERIT SCHOLARS	NUMBER OF SCHOLARS REPORTING THIS GROUP AS FATHER'S OCCUPATION, 1956	NUMBER OF MALE WORKERS REQUIRED TO PRODUCE ONE MERIT SCHOLAR
I Professional, technical, & kindred workers	234	12,672
II Managers, official proprietors	115	37,153
III Sales workers	34	77,632
IV Clerical & kindred	28	95,380
V Craftsmen, foremen, & kindred	56	140,112
VI Operatives & kindred	27	313,731
VII Service workers	7	366,270
VIII Farmers, farm managers, laborers, & foremen	16	389,643
IX Laborers, except farm & mine	1	3,581,370

Bond's study is an extraordinary comment on the influence of social class factors in the awarding of scholarships. According to these findings, a student whose father is a "professional, technical, or kindred worker" has 1 chance in 12,672 to win a Merit award, while a student whose father is a "laborer, except farm & mine" has only 1 chance in 3,581,370. This is especially significant since Merit awards, unlike most other scholarships, are given on the basis of a comprehensive nationally administered examination.

In general the most educated and most highly paid occupations are the most scholar-producing, though the top scholar-producing groups were not necessarily the most highly paid. The top five were the following.

OCCUPATION	NUMBER OF WORKERS REQUIRED TO PRODUCE ONE MERIT SCHOLAR
1. Librarians	3195
2. College presidents, professors, & instructors	3429
3. Architects	4566
4. Lawyers & judges	4861
5. Clergymen	8667

It appears, then, that among the most "scholarly" groups the correlation between income and educational achievement is not always high. In particular, librarians, clergymen, and college instructors have relatively low incomes, while at the same time having very high scholastic achievement levels. The top position of librarians raises a very interesting question, one that can be raised about scholastic standards at all educational levels, elementary school through college: Does this method of selecting award winners overemphasize bookishness at the expense of such qualities as creativity, independence, and individuality? Indications are that "intellectuality" is too often the equivalent of card-cataloguing bookishness and little else.

Failures

By contrast with the successful students, the failures were more often found in lower-income groups. The percentage

of high-school students with one or more subject failures
was as follows.

INCOME GROUP	PERCENTAGE OF FAILURE
I ($5000—)	42.2%
II ($6000—)	36.0
III ($7000—)	32.2
IV ($8000—)	28.8
V ($9000—)	28.6

These failure rates follow a regular income pattern. In
group I there were 13.6 per cent more failures than in
group V.

In Big City, social studies and English are required subjects, English for four years and social studies for three.
But, while everyone takes these subjects, not everyone
passes them, as the figures show.

Percentage of Failures

INCOME GROUP	SOCIAL STUDIES	ENGLISH
I	14.6%	16.8%
II	13.9	10.9
III	12.7	9.3
IV	10.2	8.5
V	7.9	6.6

Of the two subjects it appears that English is the more
troublesome for students in group I, and social studies the
more difficult for the other four income groups.

In English there are 10.2 per cent more failures in group
I than in group V. In social studies there are only 6.7 per
cent more failures in group I. The high failure rate in
English indicates that students in group I have special

language problems which seem to call for special attention. The language deficiency may be mainly in reading or it may be in written or oral English. It is certainly a commonplace observation that lower-income groups characteristically "don't speak good English." Oral skills of course are very largely derivative from reading skills, but they can and should be treated separately. At present there appear to be no techniques in use that are at all successful in improving the speech habits of lower-income groups.

Failures in health education were distributed as follows.

INCOME GROUP	PERCENTAGE OF FAILURE
I	9.8%
II	5.5
III	3.7
IV	4.3
V	6.5

In group I almost one out of every ten students failed health education. It might be assumed that at least in this subject low-income students would have a chance for success, but even here they frequently fail. The lowest failure rate is found in group III, while group V has a surprisingly high failure rate.

Detention School

Detention School admissions among high-school students are not quite so topheavy in the lower-income groups as they were among elementary school students. Probably this is attributable to the fact that a great many delinquent youths drop out of school before or shortly after they get to high school. Admissions per 1000 high school students in each income group were as follows.

INCOME GROUP	DETENTION SCHOOL ADMISSIONS
I ($5000—)	17.7
II ($6000—)	7.2
III ($7000—)	4.9
IV ($8000—)	3.8
V ($9000—)	4.2
A (below $7000)	13.4
B (above $7000)	4.1

It should be noted here that: 1. The proportion of students in the Detention School from group A is more than three times as great as in group B. 2. There is a disproportionately heavy concentration of students in group I, the lowest income group. 3. The rate is somewhat higher in group V than in group IV. Only further investigation can explain this interesting irregularity, but several things might be suggested as possibilities. There is only one high school in group V; since this school includes a few very underprivileged areas within its boundaries, including a relatively large Negro ghetto, many of the delinquents in this school may actually be low-income students. Or, perhaps some of the upper-income students in this school are "overprivileged," unrestrained in their behavior, and therefore more inclined to delinquency.

After-School Groups

Parent Groups

In high school as in elementary school, upper-income parents are much more active in school groups than lower-income parents. The number of parent members in school groups, per 100 students in each income group, is as follows.

INCOME GROUP	PARENT GROUP-MEMBERS
I ($5000—)	8.0
II ($6000—)	3.5
III ($7000—)	25.8
IV ($8000—)	24.6
V ($9000—)	36.0
A (below $7000)	6.2
B (above $7000)	30.8

For some unexplained reasons more parents are active in group I than in group II, but the rate of participation in group B is about five times greater than the rate in group A.

Summer School

Enrollments in summer school, per 100 students enrolled in regular school, were:

INCOME GROUP	SUMMER-SCHOOL ENROLLMENTS
I ($5000—)	71.8
II ($6000—)	60.1
III ($7000—)	63.3
IV ($8000—)	78.2
V ($9000—)	132.9
A (below $7000)	66.9
B (above $7000)	81.1

Thus the enrollment in summer school was heavier in group IV (from this and surrounding areas) than regular school enrollment.

Evening School Enrollment

Lower-income adults would seem to need further education more than upper-income adults; yet in group A (the lower-income half) enrollment in adult evening school is 26.0 per cent of day-school enrollment, while in group B it is 39.4 per cent. Enrollment in group B is therefore more than half again as great as in group A.

Meetings

For a fee, community groups may use high-school buildings as meeting places. The fee is not large, but no adjustment is made based on ability to pay. The distribution of permits to use school buildings was:

INCOME GROUP	AVERAGE NO. OF PERMITS PER SCHOOL
I ($5000—)	19
II ($6000—)	26
III ($7000—)	42
IV ($8000—)	58
V ($9000—)	62
A (below $7000)	22
B (above $7000)	50

Thus more than twice as many permits were issued per school in group B as in group A.

Extracurricular Activities

Extracurricular activities are mainly club activities which take place outside of the regular academic curriculum. Since these activities are voluntary, non-credit, and quite time-consuming, they provide a good indication of how much student interest there is in school. Usually only "successful" students, those who feel some attachment for the school, become members of school clubs; those who feel alienated and have no sense of belonging rarely join.

Some of these club activities are related to school subjects—drama, Latin, science, etc. Others are merely social and recreational. Many bear a close resemblance to the fraternities and sororities which have been outlawed in the state for many years because of what is claimed to be their snobbish and undemocratic character. Some clubs have more status than others, though membership in almost all of them involves a rather high level of social acceptability.

Unfortunately no information in usable form was available about club activities in Big City schools. Information is available from other sources and other school systems, however, and it is perhaps not unreasonable to infer that there are many parallels in Big City schools.

Professor Hollingshead, for example, discovered that upper-class students in Elmtown high school tended to dominate the school's extracurricular activities, with participation rates as follows. (His numbering system proceeds from "highest" to "lowest" class groups and is the reverse of ours.) [2]

SOCIAL CLASS (highest to lowest)		PERCENTAGE OF STUDENTS IN EXTRACURRICULAR ACTIVITIES
Highest classes	I & II	100.0%
	III	75.3
	IV	57.4
Lowest class	V	27.0

All students in the two upper classes belonged to school groups, as compared with only 27 per cent in the lowest

class. One of the "lower-class" girls talked about club activities in the high school in rather blunt language: "We
are pushed out of things. There is a group of girls here
who think they are higher than us. They look down on us.
I won't mention any names, but they are a group of girls
from the higher families. They have a club that is supposed to be outside of school, but it's really in the school.
They just go from one club to the other and hog all of
the offices. They snub us and they won't talk to us. I'd like
to be in the school activities and the school plays, go to
the dances, and things like that, but they make us feel
like we're not wanted."

The situation in Big City schools may not be as bad as
this. Since Big City has seventeen high schools and Elmtown only one, the mixture of income groups and the social
distance between students may be greater in Elmtown
than in many Big City schools.

From all appearances, snobbery and exclusiveness seem
to be particularly prevalent in the upper-income high
schools of Big City. Recently a young girl who was a student at the highest-income school in the city disappeared
from her home, leaving a diary of complaints about snobbery in the school. The girl's parents had emigrated to
Big City from Britain. Newspaper reports described her
father as a shoe salesman, and the family's economic position apparently was significantly below "norm" for the
area. After a period of many days (during which the whole
city was alerted to her absence), she was found wander-
ing in a field, apparently deranged by her experience.
During and shortly after this incident, there was much
local discussion about the system of social exclusion in
the high school which may have contributed to, caused,

or perhaps precipitated this student's breakdown. The discussion has now ended and the system continues as before.

S. Abrahamson also studied the operation of the school social system—in six different communities—and concluded: "Participation in extracurricular activities in a school program acts as a reward in that the students involved in the activities develop a deeper sense of appreciation for school, a higher level of morale, and a keen feeling of sharing in the school program. . . . The higher the social class background of the students, the more they tended to participate in extracurricular activities." [3]

Abrahamson found that no lower-lower-class students in these six communities held any elected offices and that upper-lower-class students held less than one-third of their rightful share. On the other hand, upper-middle-class students held about three times their rightful share.

In general, upper-class students tend to be popular because they are more "socially acceptable"; they tend to be well dressed and well cared for; their status position gives them confidence, social poise, and the manners that go with "good breeding." They have spending money and nice homes in which to entertain friends. They are usually successful in their school work and seldom disgruntled and rebellious. Popularity seems to be only their "natural due," though in truth it appears to be due mainly to the class and status position of their families.

In the Emporia, Kansas, senior high school, R. Durham and C. S. Cole found that over a six-year period the upper class constituted 7.9 per cent of the total student body, while holding the following percentages of offices and club memberships. [4]

Important Leaders	29.2%
Student Council Members	21.7
Senior Honor Group	18.0
Club Members	21.2

In a sense, club activities are the social equivalents of "gifted"-child programs. The function, though perhaps not the purpose, of both programs is to provide special services to upper-income groups. At the same time, in so far as they suffer the psychological consequences of being left out or relegated to an inferior status, lower-income students seem to get less than nothing out of either program.

The Selecting and Sorting Process

Subjects Studied

In elementary schools all students study essentially the same subjects; in high schools, because of the variety of curriculums and elective subjects, they tend to pursue different studies. This "open range" of subjects is the basis of the selecting and sorting process in the high school, a process which prepares some students for professional and managerial careers, some for white-collar and "vocational" jobs, and others for nothing much at all.

Subjects studied in high school tend to vary with social class position, as indicated in Table 15.

Among the significant items in this table are these: Enrollment in health education is 14.8 per cent heavier in group A (below $7000) than in group B.

The home economics enrollment varies in almost strict

TABLE 15. Big City Enrollments in Various Subjects
(percentage of total number of students in
each income group)

INCOME GROUP	HEALTH EDUCATION	HOME ECONOMICS	INDUSTRIAL EDUCATION	MATH	MUSIC	RETAILING
I	61.0%	19.4%	29.1%	43.7%	23.5%	2.3%
II	62.2	17.0	39.0	32.8	17.3	3.1
III	57.2	11.7	34.5	56.7	14.6	1.8
IV	44.3	12.7	24.5	62.8	22.8	3.6
V	46.2	4.6	15.7	66.5	9.8	3.7
A	62.3	18.5	32.1	40.2	20.9	2.2
B	49.5	11.2	26.5	61.4	18.0	2.3

INCOME GROUP	ART	BUSINESS EDUCATION	FAMILY LIVING	FOREIGN LANGUAGE	SCIENCE	ROTC
I	11.2%	73.2%	4.3%	12.5%	45.5%	7.1%
II	8.4	88.4	2.8	16.7	50.7	7.7
III	10.3	67.4	2.9	24.1	44.1	4.6
IV	10.7	54.5	4.5	29.4	44.1	3.5
V	7.9	37.1	3.0	52.5	56.5	3.1
A	9.8	79.9	3.7	14.2	46.7	7.6
B	10.5	57.8	3.2	30.8	45.0	3.1

accordance with income, a big drop-off occurring in group
V, where families are likely to hire domestic help to do
home chores.

Industrial education enrollments also vary in accordance
with income, except that enrollments in group I are unusually low. This lowest income group tends to be excluded
from the skilled trades and also to have poor industrial education facilities in its schools.

Enrollment in business education (shorthand, typing,
etc.) is unusually high in group II. Apparently many stu-

dents in this group plan to work in secretarial and white-collar jobs.

Group V enrollments in foreign language are extremely high.

Enrollments in math are 21.2 per cent higher in group B than in group A.

Enrollments in science are higher in the lower-income groups than would be expected, but the highest enrollment percentage is found in group V.

Comparing the lowest and the highest income groups, we find that group I is heavily enrolled in health education, home economics, music, art, business education, family living, and ROTC. Group V, on the other hand, is heavily enrolled in "academic" subjects—foreign language, math, and science. The other income groups seem to be enrolled in subjects in accordance with their own special occupational destinations.

One of the liveliest and longest-standing disputes in education concerns high-school electives. Some argue that all students should study essentially the same subjects, much as they do in elementary school; others argue that students should have more electives and a broader range of choices. The pros and cons of the argument run about as follows.

More choice: Students are all different; they have different interests, aptitudes, and occupational plans. Therefore they should all study different subjects. In Big City high schools, English, social studies and some math and science are now required of all students; this is enough "standardization," perhaps more than enough.

Less choice: Students are more nearly equal in their aptitudes and potential than most people assume and should share more common experiences. Many have no "occupational plans" other than what counselors or teachers have suggested. Variety in curriculum offerings results in students' being "guided" into paths which perpetuate social class origins. Moreover, students find a wide range of electives more confusing than rewarding.

The argument is carried on in different ways and at various levels, usually does not involve an extremist either-or position. It is more a matter of the direction in which we should proceed from our present position—whether toward more electives or toward more "standardization."

Both sides argue persuasively but, at the present time in Big City, it appears that there are too many elective offerings and too much premature type-casting of students. Obviously culturally deprived students have different academic needs from those of culturally privileged students. But what they need, mainly, is more attention, not an inferior or "vocational" curriculum. Little evidence exists to support the assumption that these students cannot master "academic" subjects or that they are "fit only for manual labor and unskilled jobs." In so far as their high-school training is different from that of upper-income groups, it should be mainly training which repairs deficiencies in their backgrounds so that they can compete on more nearly equal terms with upper-income groups. It should go without saying, however, that the "academic" offerings, to upper- and lower-income groups alike, should be sensible, meaningful, and interesting. In Big City most students in low-income groups are being prepared for low-income jobs, as the following material on curriculum enrollments makes clear.

Curriculum Enrollment

Not all school systems separate students into different curriculums in high school. A school system adjacent to Big City, which has a reputation for being one of the best in the country, does not make curriculum separations at all, but simply guides students into various subjects according to their interests. This system is typical of many throughout the country.

Big City, however, makes these curriculum separations. All high schools in the city offer three distinct courses of study, or curriculums: college preparatory, general, and business-and-vocational. The business-and-vocational curriculum is designed for those students who plan to work in offices or in the trades, skilled or semi-skilled. The general curriculum is designed for those who do not seem to fit anywhere else. Most of the students who enroll in this curriculum will eventually become unskilled workers.

Since students are usually only fourteen when they enter high school (fifteen if they enter from junior high school), the decision to enter a fixed curriculum, with its occupational limitations, seems very premature. What is more, the decision seems unnecessary. A student who wants to prepare for college can take suitable courses without being put in a special curriculum and segregated from students in other curriculums. In fact, all students could be processed through high school on the assumption that they might some day want to go to college. At fourteen most students know little about college or about the occupational possibilities open to them. They are too young to make an informed and free choice of curriculums; as a consequence the choice is very heavily influenced, if not actually made in most cases, by teachers and counselors and, in upper-income groups especially, by parents.

Considering the accelerated tempo of technological change and the resulting changes in the nature of work assignments, it may be doubted that schools can successfully train students for particular work assignments. Certainly employers would prefer potential employees who are literate rather than partially trained in an already outmoded "vocational" skill. Consequently, it would seem wiser to concentrate on "general" education at all levels.

By the school's own standards, curriculum choices are very often misguided. Professor Samuel A. Stouffer says: "A nation-wide survey shows that among seniors in the top 30 per cent of ability, a third of the boys and nearly half of the girls were not, at the time of the survey, in college preparatory courses." [5] Curriculum assignments are often made on the basis of social class factors; again, Stouffer says: "It is known, for example, that even very able boys from working-class homes who fail to make really good grades in the seventh and eighth grades are seldom advised to take a college preparatory course. This is not equally true of boys from white-collar homes."

Indications of the influence of social class on curriculum assignments are shown in Table 16.

Almost half the students in group I are enrolled in the free-floating general curriculum. This is five times the enrollment in group V.

Only 19 per cent of students in group I are enrolled in college preparatory; in group V, 79 per cent are enrolled.

Enrollments in all three curriculums follow a regular income pattern in the major income groups. The only ex-

TABLE 16. Curriculum Enrollments
Percentage of students in each school

INCOME GROUP	COLLEGE PREPARATORY	BUSINESS AND VOCATIONAL	GENERAL
1 $5000—	15%	30%	55%
2	19	41	40
3	16	27	57
4	18	27	55
5	25	40	34
6 $6000—	25	40	35
7	15	60	25
8	34	39	27
9 $7000—	33	35	32
10	54	23	24
11	37	33	30
12	35	34	31
13 $8000—	50	25	25
14	59	17	24
15	53	22	25
16	64	19	17
17 $9000—	79	11	10
I ($5000—)	19	33	48
II ($6000—)	25	46	29
III ($7000—)	40	31	29
IV ($8000—)	57	21	23
V ($9000—)	79	11	10

ception is the unusually heavy enrollment of group II in the business and vocational curriculum.

In interpreting college-preparatory enrollments it should be kept in mind that many of the group V students enrolled in non-college curriculums are probably lower-income students who "happen" to attend this highest-income high school, and that well over half the students in

lower-income groups drop out of school before graduation. Thus is cannot be said that 19 per cent of *all* group
I students take college-preparatory courses. Counting drop-
outs, and considering the curriculums the drop-outs would
have been enrolled in, the percentage would be much
lower than this.

What effect does enrollment in one or another of these
curriculums have on a student's chances for social and academic success? One senior high-school girl quoted in Hollingshead's Elmtown study claimed that enrollment in
the college-preparatory curriculum was the key to success
in high school.

> If you take a college preparatory course, you're better than
> those who take a general course. Those who take a general
> course are neither here nor there. If you take a commercial
> course, you don't rate. It's a funny thing, those who take col-
> lege preparatory set themselves up as better than the other
> kids. Those that take the college preparatory course run the
> place.
> I remember when I was a freshman mother wanted me to
> take home economics, but I didn't want to. I knew I couldn't
> rate. You could take typing and shorthand and still rate, but
> if you took a straight commercial course, you couldn't rate.
> You see, you're rated by the teachers according to the course
> you take. They rate you in the first six weeks. The teachers
> type you in a small school and you're made in classes before
> you get there. College prep. kids get good grades and the
> others take what's left. The teachers get together and talk,
> and if you are not in college prep. you haven't got a chance.[6]

From long experience with the situation, we suspect
that approximately the same prestige attaches to the

college-preparatory curriculum in Big City; those who are "in" are usually enrolled in college prep, and those who are "out" are usually in general or vocational curriculums.

Through the use of separate curriculums and other devices, including segregated groupings of various sorts, the schools establish a class system which is more rigid in its way than the class system in the outside world, since all students have curriculum and "ability" labels which segregate them from other students in a clearly defined rank order. In this school social system, the college preparatory curriculum is the upper class, the vocational curriculum the middle, and the general curriculum the lowest class. Within this class structure there is apparently little movement either up or down. Once assigned to a curriculum and status level in the high school, students seldom change to other curriculums and class categories.

This curriculum-class system is neither necessary nor inevitable, since, as has been noted, numbers of high-ranking school systems do not make these distinctions at all. It is observed in *Who Shall Be Educated?* that "one of the more significant social experiments of our time is being carried on in a number of city high schools in the Middle West and West." In these schools "all students are in a single curriculum, with many individual electives, but without hard and fast divisions into college-preparatory, commercial, vocational, etc." The consequence of this system is that there are "no divisions on the basis of which claims to social status can be made. All kinds of students are in the same English, mathematics and history courses, regardless of their college-going intentions." [7]

The system is not equally popular with all elements in the community, however. "The schools in these cities are

criticized by many upper-middle-class people because they
do not have 'high standards' and do not 'prepare well for
college.' Yet a comprehensive and careful study of the
college records of students from several of these schools
shows that in college they do as well as or better than do the
graduates from traditional college-preparatory curricula
and traditional high schools with a college-preparatory
emphasis."

"It is probable," the authors conclude, "that the criticisms coming from upper-middle-class people come in part
from uneasiness over the threatened disintegration of
social-status lines in the high school with the disappearance
of clearly marked differences among curricula."

Naturally these "upper-middle-class criticisms" cannot
be regarded as legitimate objections to the single-cur-
riculum system. On the contrary they seem to argue in
favor of it, for in a democratic society we cannot justify
giving artificial support to the status claims of upper-
class groups. As an instrument of democracy, the schools
should work to reduce class barriers rather than to rein-
force them. The single curriculum therefore seems fairer,
just as efficient, and much more in keeping with democratic
goals than the class-curriculum system now used in Big
City and elsewhere. Yet no audible criticisms have been
made in Big City of the system, and some people are
prepared to go even further than curriculum divisions.
The citizens' committee recommended in its final report
that all high-school diplomas awarded to students in the
city should "include a notation of the school from which
the student has graduated and the curriculum com-
pleted." Thus students are to bear class labels not only
in school but presumably for the rest of their lives.

Who Goes to College?

It seems safe to assume that all, or nearly all, students who were in the college-prep curriculum will at least *try* to go to college. Many who try will not succeed. And many who succeed will not last out the first semester.

College drop-outs among lower-income students are reported to be very high, though exact figures are not available. In the state university located inside Big City (attended at least in the freshman year by numbers of lower-income students) about *one-third* of all registered students drop out in their first year.[8] An undetermined number return and finish school.

No doubt large numbers of these drop-outs are lower-income students. A study conducted at the university shows "financial difficulties" to be the most common cause of drop-out, with "lack of interest in studies" coming in second.

Though drop-out, even when students later return, would seem to indicate serious problems of an economic, emotional, or academic nature, colleges seem as unconcerned about the problems involved as the public schools seem to be.

For those who can hang on, college attendance means a great deal—good jobs, higher pay, an enriched life, and higher status. In a sense, college attendance is the most important element in class structure. Indeed, Vance Packard advances the theory in *The Status Seekers* that college attendance is now the most decisive factor in separating the "Haves" from the "Have Nots" in modern society.[9]

The only relevant information available in Big City about college attendance had to do with the number of students in Big City "requesting transcripts for college," and the educational and occupational plans of high-school graduates.

The percentage of students requesting transcripts of their high-school credits in order to apply for college admission was as follows.

I ($5000—)	22.8%
II ($6000—)	34.0
III ($7000—)	46.3
IV ($8000—)	60.6
V ($9000—)	81.0
A (below $7000)	27.0
B (above $7000)	57.4

According to these figures there is a difference of 58.2 per cent between groups I and V in the percentage of students applying for college. The percentage figure in group B (the upper-income half) is more than twice as great as in group A.

Responses to a survey of Big City high-school graduates about their future plans revealed the information shown in Table 17. (Some students had no plans and checked only the "Further Counseling Wanted" category; some checked "Job Promised" as well as other categories.)

It may be seen in this table that the percentage of students planning to go to college "immediately" increases as income increases, with a great forward leap in group V. The percentage in group V is more than three times greater than in group I.

In group I, 60 per cent of the graduates feel they need further counseling from the schools—almost twice the percentage found in group V.

TABLE 17. After Graduation

INCOME GROUP	COLLEGE IMME- DIATELY	WORK— COLLEGE LATER	WORK PERMA- NENTLY	JOB PROMISED	FURTHER COUNSELING WANTED
I ($5000—)	27%	36%	26%	5%	60%
II ($6000—)	32	18	41	13	57
III ($7000—)	43	14	33	11	47
IV ($8000—)	57	12	26	18	53
V ($9000—)	87	5	6	23	35
A (below $7000)	28	29	32	8	59
B (above $7000)	55	14	26	16	48

Almost one out of every four graduates in group V already has a job promised, though they have not yet started college. In this group, 92 per cent of the graduates plan to enter college either now or later. The percentage in the other major income groups with plans for college *now or later* is:

INCOME GROUP	PERCENTAGE PLANNING FOR COLLEGE
I ($5000—)	63%
II ($6000—)	50
III ($7000—)	57
IV ($8000—)	69
V ($9000—)	92

It is most interesting that 63 per cent of all graduates in group I *want* to go to college at some time or another. Possible explanations for this might be:

One: High-school graduates in group I are much more highly selected than those at other income levels. Drop-outs in this lowest-income group are so heavy that only unusually serious and determined students remain in school long enough to graduate, the social and economic pressures to leave school being what they are in the lower-income environment. We could expect, then, that many of those who graduate from high school would have enough interest in education at least to *want* to go to college.

Of course most of those in the "Work—College Later" category will probably never get to college. Their desire to go may in fact represent quite unrealistic job and educational aspirations, which may lead to final disappointment.

Two: It is so difficult for students in this lowest-income group to find jobs, much less desirable jobs, that going to college is often the only way out for them. Some evidence of the job scarcity for lower-income youths is found in the "Job Promised" column of Table 17. While a total of 62 per cent of group I students plan to work after high-school graduation, only 5 per cent have jobs promised; at the same time 11 per cent of students in the highest-income groups plan to work immediately, yet 23 per cent of them have jobs promised.

Three: Related to point two, very low-income groups are often denied job opportunities because of racial and class factors. For example, either because of prejudice or lack of "know how," individuals from these groups rarely enter business or the skilled trades. Often the best way for them to get "better jobs" is through education for the professions or white-collar and government service.

Again an illustration can be taken from the "Job Promised" column. Jobs are usually promised in the business or trade of the father or other relatives. The fact that few jobs have been promised to group I students indicates that they probably do not have relatives in business or trade and that these avenues of escape tend, therefore, to be closed to them.

Why does college attendance (or the likely prospect) vary in almost strict accord with family income? All the social class factors discussed in this study provide possible answers to this question. Those which may be especially pertinent are: [10]

One: College is expensive, even for many upper-income families. For lower-income families the costs are usually prohibitive. The average annual expense of college students (unmarried undergraduates, 1959–60) is $1550. Of this amount, most is paid out of the parents' pockets—$950, or about 61 per cent of the total. Students themselves contribute an average of only $360 toward college expenses. Scholarships provide only $130, on the average—or about 8 per cent of the total costs. Perhaps because college is largely a parental expense, and a costly one, college students are recruited mainly from upper-income families, those who can afford to pay. Among families above the $10,000 income bracket, 95 per cent with children under ten expect them to attend college. This bracket now sends 70 per cent of its eighteen-to-nineteen-year-olds to college. Among families earning $5000 to $7500, 80 per cent aspire to college, and only 40 per cent get there. In the lowest-income bracket, among families earning less than $3000 a year, 40 per cent would like to attend, and only 20 per cent manage to do so. Undoubtedly college drop-outs among this 20 per cent are numerous, judging by the heavy drop-outs in state colleges attended by lower-income students.

Often lower-income students will be admitted to college, yet fail to appear at registration time. In Big City, over *one-fourth* of all students admitted to the state university in the city failed to enroll in classes, either there or elsewhere. Study revealed that, on an average, this vanished group had somewhat better admission qualifications than those finally admitted. "Thus they had good potentiality for college work. *Inability to finance collegiate work* proved to be a significant factor for a large majority of them."

Of course scholarships are available—some half-million of them—but they tend to go to higher-income students. Those from lower-income families either do not meet the standards, do not apply, or cannot afford to go to college, even with scholarship money.

At no college subscribing to the College Scholarship Service (mostly high-prestige colleges) do as many as half the scholarship winners come from the neediest half of our nation's population.

It is estimated that the median income of the scholarship holder's family is between $6000 and $7000 a year, as compared with a national median of $5000 per family. The figures, interestingly, are largely estimates, since very few colleges keep family income records.

A recent study of two hundred selected colleges puts the figures for applicants even higher. According to this report, the median family income of scholarship *applicants* was almost $7500. Nearly one-third had incomes over $8000, and one out of ten had incomes over $12,000. At the same time, only one out of ten applicants had incomes below $4000. Thus lower-income students are unlikely even to make application for scholarship money.

The *New York Times* comments about these figures:

"Admissions officers are much concerned over what they regard as the serious implications of these figures, for the colleges, for the nation's youth, and for the national welfare. These figures, some of them say, reflect forces inducing a kind of collegiate segregation, which will be accentuated as college fees rise, as they are continuing to do." [11]

According to the director of the College Scholarship Service, Rexford G. Moon, Jr., the nation is now losing the talents of 150,000 able youths a year from the lower-income levels, or three-quarters of all the able students who for one reason or another do not continue their education beyond high school.[12]

Dean Munro of Harvard wants colleges to "stop making scholarship awards for embellishment purposes to well-off students." He also thinks that college representatives should explore the whole field. "Why should three hundred college representatives visit New Trier High School each year and hardly any, except coaches, visit the big downtown Chicago high school only twenty miles away?" At the present time, of the nation's 26,500 high schools, a mere 5000 produce 82 per cent of all college students.

The big need, Munro says, is for coordination of the college talent hunters. Plaut of the National Scholarship Service and Fund for Negro Students has recently urged a national program, costing up to $100 million, for developing the neglected talents of Negro and other underprivileged children.

Of course, college admission is easier now than it used to be for lower-income students, and class distinctions are not as exaggerated as they once were. Today, including

all part-time students, 20.6 per cent * of all youths eighteen
to twenty-one are in colleges and universities in this
country. The doors of higher education have opened
somewhat and permitted a relatively small inflow of the
underprivileged.

In John Adams' day at Harvard matters were worse.
Students were graded according to family social standing,
and if the student's father was a man of power and position,
the son was ranked first and given the head seat at the
table, the best room, the first place in academic processions,
the privilege of helping himself first in the commons.

Harvard today is not that bad, but in all honesty it's
not very much better. The class distinctions are simply
less obvious and objectionable. Though Harvard, rich and
lavish with its scholarships, is perhaps the most "democratic" of the Ivy Leaguers, only 18 per cent of its *scholarship* students come from families with less than $4000 in-
come (not much below the national median).

Two: Lower-income students usually lack even the
crudest information about such simple matters as how to
prepare for college, which college to choose, how to get in,
how to get along, once in, how to fill out acceptable ap-
plications. They don't have the "know how" of the upper-
income student. Their parents and friends, typically, have
not been to college or even inside a college classroom.
Thus they cannot give directions or show them the way.
The upper-income student, on the other hand, learns the

* This figure represents a careful recalculation by Bernard Berelson (*The
Graduate School in the United States*) of previous estimates which have
generally overstated college enrollment, some putting it as high as 40
per cent of those of college age. Comparable figures from other countries
are not available. Indications are, however, that enrollment in the USSR
is roughly comparable, and that the rate of increase there is more rapid.

way from his parents, who have usually been there before. He is headed in the right direction early in his life, equipped with a rather complete blueprint of the route to school success.

The lack of "know how" among lower-income groups was recently illustrated in the author's own experience. A semi-skilled factory worker consulted the author about the possibility of his son's going to college. He wanted to know how his son should go about applying, whether he should write or call, to whom he should talk, what schools there were in the area, etc.

The questions were posed in such a simple and puzzled sort of way that it seemed almost as though he were inquiring about how to get to the moon, the distances and the difficulties of the trip appearing to be equally great. The upper-income parent would probably know the answers to these questions, and a great deal more, out of his own experience. And not only would he be able to guide his son into college admittance, he would also be able to counsel him about the hundreds of problems that trouble students during the course of their college careers. The lower-income student who manages somehow to get into college often hangs on there by a thin thread; perhaps more often than not the thread breaks and the student drops out in his first semester. The pace of college life is fast, and human relations are very impersonal; if a student does not know the way and has no one to show him, the thread will often break at the first sign of strain. As we have mentioned, the drop-out rate among lower-income college students is reported to reach disaster proportions during the first semester of attendance. These students don't know how to go to college; their failure to get along is so tragic for them and so wasteful of human resources (not to mention school resources) as to demand intensive study and attention.

Many people claim that it is not social class, the ability to pay, or parental counseling that makes the difference in college attendance, but intelligence. Low-income students do not go to college, they say, because they are not intelligent enough; upper-income students go to college, and are successful there, because they have "superior" intelligence.

Using their own intelligence-measuring tool—the IQ test—let us examine this argument.

Joseph A. Kahl tabulated the IQ scores and father's occupation of 3348 boys who expected to go to college.[13] He discovered that in the highest occupational group (Major White Collar), 56 per cent of boys in the *lowest* IQ fifth expected to go to college. In the lowest occupational group (Other Labor and Service) only 9 per cent of boys in the lowest fifth expected to attend college.

At the other extreme, in the highest occupational group, 89 per cent of boys in the *highest* IQ fifth had college expectations, while only 29 per cent of boys in the same group whose fathers were in the lowest occupations had such expectations. The complete list is shown in Table 18.

From these data it seems very clear that college expectations depend much more on the occupation of the father than on the student's IQ score.

Kahl also interviewed twenty-four "common-man" boys. All these boys had high IQ scores but only half of them planned to enter college. The following observations from

TABLE 18. Percentage of Boys Who Expect to Go to College

FATHER'S OCCUPATION	LOWEST IQ QUINTILE	HIGHEST IQ QUINTILE
Major White Collar	56%	89%
Middle White Collar	28	76
Minor White Collar	12	55
Skilled Labor & Service	4	40
Other Labor & Service	9	29

these interviews help explain some of the difficulties these boys have with school and with plans for higher education. "There were no cases," Kahl says, "in which the boy found in school work sufficient intellectual satisfactions to supply its own motivation. And there were no cases where a sympathetic and encouraging teacher had successfully stimulated a boy to higher aspiration. School and the possibility of college were viewed by all the boys solely as steps to jobs. None was interested in learning for the subtle pleasures it can offer; none craved intellectual understanding for its own sake."

One boy, who got the best marks in his class, summed up his attitude toward school. "I don't hate school, but I don't think there are many who are dying to go. I'll be glad when I get through."

For these "common-man" boys, advancing education offered a special problem—homework. "When homework first appeared (around the eighth grade), it became a question of homework vs. baseball, homework vs. day-dreaming, homework vs. after-school job that brought in precious money and independence from father's pocketbook. Before this time, it was easy for a bright boy to do well: spontaneous intellectual curiosity was all the teacher asked. Homework was a different matter.

"A boy would sacrifice other pleasures for homework when they weren't important to him. If a boy was not good at sports, if he did not have close and satisfying peer contacts, or if he had no hobby that was strongly rewarding as well as distracting, then the cost of homework was less and the balance more in its favor. In extreme cases, frustrations in these alternative spheres motivated a boy to good school performance as compensation."

Kahl also interviewed the parents of these boys and found that some parents did not feel they should push their sons in the direction of college. One mother's comments were:

> I don't go to see the teachers. I figure the teachers know what they're doing. When I go up there I can't talk good enough. Some women go up there, and I don't know, they're so la-ti-ta. But I can't talk that way. Me, I'm just plain words of one syllable and that's all. And the teachers, they'd just as soon not have you get in their way, I figure. They know what they're doing. . . . I hate to push the kid. I figure he'll get his knocks later on, and should do what he wants to now. . . . I don't make them do homework or anything. I figure they're old enough to know what they want to do and they'll get their work done by and by.

Professor S. A. Stouffer says that parental attitudes toward school and parental educational levels are often decisive in college attendance, and that white-collar workers are more likely than blue-collar workers with similar (or even higher) incomes to send their children to college.[14]

Of course comparisons of blue- and white-collar incomes can be very deceptive since blue-collar income is subject to sharp decline during lay-off periods. It seems likely, however, that college attendance would be more difficult for students from blue-collar families, if for no other reason than that blue-collar workers seem less intent on climbing up the social class ladder into professional jobs. Also, as Stouffer says, parents in working-class neighborhoods "usually have no conception of college as a goal for their children, even their very bright children. Those who do have such a concept often fail to motivate their child, because of ineptness or because the alternative attractions of nonschool-oriented peer groups in the neighborhood are too enticing for the boy or girl to overcome."

He also refers to the importance of ethnic background in college attendance, pointing specifically to what he terms the "amazing success" of Jewish students in school, almost regardless of income. Other ethnic groups also tend to excel in school, notably Armenians and Japanese-Americans, among others. In these ethnic groups education is highly prized, and scholarship, especially at the college level, is heavily emphasized. So it can be said that, within *any* income group, some ethnic sub-groups will do better in school than others, as will some white-collar and other occupational groups. College attendance, then, will be closely related to family income with some ethnic and occupational group variations.

Graduate education, apparently, is a somewhat different matter. Those who go on to the highest levels of education (the graduate school) do not necessarily come from the most privileged groups. Berelson found that, while 38 per cent of Ph.D. recipients in his survey had fathers who had also attended college, 32 per cent had fathers with less than a high-school education. Occupational levels, however, tended to be higher. Almost half had fathers who worked in professional, business, or technical occupations. Only 6 per cent of the fathers of these Ph.D.s were unskilled workers. By contrast, two-thirds to three-fourths of law and medical students came from business, managerial, or proprietary families. Berelson comments: "It is hard to overstate the importance of the graduate school to students of high talent but low origin—and especially those from an ethnic minority traditionally devoted to learning."

"Ability" Groups

The schools employ various means of segregating students. In addition to curriculum divisions, "ability" grouping is another commonly used segregation device.

This device is used to some extent at the elementary-school level, where students are often grouped somewhat informally according to teacher-rated "ability" in subjects such as reading and arithmetic; in some schools there is a growing tendency to separate students into different home-room groups on this basis.

At the high-school level, "ability" groupings often become highly formalized and systematized. It is very difficult to get exact information about these groups. No records are kept in Big City concerning their use, and administrators seem reluctant to discuss them—either because they do not know much about them or because they regard the subject as too sensitive. According to the best reports, however, all high schools in Big City use "ability" groupings, some more than others.

One high school in the city (school number 10) uses a system that results in almost complete segregation of the various "ability" groups. When a student enters this high school he is assigned to a home room on the basis of his rated "ability" (IQ, marks, etc.). He stays with this home room throughout most of his school career. He attends classes almost exclusively with the other members of his home-room group, and it is only when he begins taking elective subjects that he has any real contact with other students in the school. In effect, he is almost completely isolated socially and intellectually from students in other "ability" groups.

This is about as complete and rigid a system of segregation as can be found in Big City schools. In view of the close relationship between "ability" ratings and social class position, these separations result in a system of social class segregation as well as a presumed system of "ability" grouping. (We hasten to add that, in this case, these groupings do not result in racial segregation, since there are very few non-whites in this school.)

Segregation in other schools in the city is not so complete, apparently, as it is in school 10. All schools in groups IV and V however use rather rigid systems, while none of the schools in groups I, II, and III (except school 10) are reported to put heavy emphasis on "ability" segregation. It appears, then, that this type of segregation, like curriculum segregation, is most popular with upper-income groups, perhaps because of their desire to prevent contact with lower-income students in the same school. At any rate almost all the demand for segregation of this kind has come traditionally from upper-income groups.

Because no information was available, it was not possible to examine the social class composition of "ability" groups in Big City schools. Judging by the "ability" ratings used in the schools, it seems inevitable that lower-income children would be assigned to lower-ranking groups and upper-income children to higher-ranking groups. This distribution has been observed in other school systems. Lloyd Warner, for example, found that each grade in Old City schools was divided into three sections, A, B, and C, according to rated "ability." Over a three-year period an analysis of the social class positions of 103 girls revealed that, of the 10 "upper-class" girls, eight were in section A (the highest ability group), one in B, and one in C. Of the 53 "lower-class" girls, only 6 were in section A, 28 in section B, and 19 in section C.[15]

Factors other than "ability" entered into the group assignments, as one of the teachers in Old City observed.

> Of course, we do some shifting around. There are some borderliners who were shifted up to make the sections more nearly even. But the socialites who aren't keeping up their standard in the A section were never taken into B or C section and they never will. They don't belong there socially. Of course, there are some girls in A section who don't belong there socially, but almost every one of the socialites is in A.
>
> Sections are supposed to be made up just on the basis of records in school but it isn't and everybody knows it isn't. I know right in my own A section I have children who ought to be in B section, but they are little socialites and so they stay in A.

And so it is that family background and all the symbols of social class inevitably count for something when honors are being awarded by the schools and when status assignments are being made. They may not always count as much as they do in Old City, but it appears that they always count.

Warner describes the effect (or perhaps the intention) of educational segregation: "The school, besides purveying knowledge to the children, keeps or helps to keep the children in groups according to social class. Thus, children learn to like being with people of their own class or higher and to dislike being with people of lower classes."

Despite the undesirable consequences of segregation, the citizens' committee in Big City recommended that "ability" groups be continued and extended. It was also recommended that the schools "identify the more able students as early as possible and make provision for advanced work." These recommendations were made even though, in a report to the citizens' committee, this statement of doubt was made about the value of "ability" groupings: "Under the impact of current criticism of education, additional impetus is being given to homogeneous grouping. The sad fact remains, however, that there is little definitive research to indicate that gifted children learn more in homogeneous groups . . . than they would learn in well-taught, undivided groups."

The tendency to segregate students at increasingly early ages seems especially dangerous. Very young children are easily molded to form. If they are put in "slow" groups, they will *be* slow, since this is expected of them, and each semester they will fall further behind the "fast" groups which are moving ahead at an accelerated pace.

We do not wish to minimize the problems teachers sometimes have in adjusting course work to a single group of students operating at different achievement levels. Under present classroom conditions, this is undeniably a deeply troublesome problem for teachers and students alike. But segregation, we would suggest, is not the answer. Perhaps a new solution can be found which will permit all students to move ahead at their own individual pace, with help and encouragement for those who have trouble and fall behind.

Lacking such a solution, which would provide for individual rather than group progress, perhaps a more flexible system of "ability" groupings can be settled on, where need is obvious and where consequences cannot be damaging.

A more flexible system would group children on a temporary basis in *each* subject. Thus a child might be in one group in reading, a second group in arithmetic, and still a third group in writing. The weakness of such systems is, however, that the child who is at one level in one subject tends to be at the same level in most other subjects. As a result, the system proves to be more rigid than it might appear. Also, it often becomes much more permanent than originally intended, as students tend to remain in assigned groups.

In addition, such systems can impose extra burdens on teachers, who must then contend with perhaps three distinct "classes" or subgroups within a class, each of which requires separate texts, tests, and lesson plans.

Some schools have tried to solve the problem of heterogeneous class groupings by using remedial teachers instead of "ability" groups. In this system the student having trouble with his lesson is given individual remedial aid during each class period by teachers specially assigned to this job. He is not put into a "slow group" where he may get little or no extra attention. Instead, his individual learning needs are attended to so that he may keep up with the rest of his group.

Interestingly, as will be noted elsewhere, Soviet schools do not use ability groupings. They tend to focus instead on a totally different solution. In the Soviet school the child who finishes his work quickly is given the responsibility of helping the child who is having trouble with his lesson. By this means one child is given experience in leadership, service to others, and the familiarity with subject matter that only a teacher acquires, while the other is given the needed help with his lessons. Also, older students in the school are often given responsibility for helping younger students who require extra help and attention.

Students themselves can obviously be a valuable source of assistance to the classroom teacher. They are in fact a great untapped source of remedial aid for children with learning problems, and perhaps even with emotional problems. It would seem that special efforts should be made to tap these rich resources.

Drop-outs

A drop-out is a student who does not graduate from high school. He presents a greater challenge to the schools and to society than the "gifted" child. Yet, perhaps because he is typically a lower-income child whose family makes few demands of the schools, he is given very little special attention. At the same time the "gifted" child, who is typically from an upper-income family, is being virtually deluged with attention in school.

The drop-out is a greater challenge because he is harder

to reach and because the schools do not have as much time to reach him. When he drops out of school, usually in the ninth or tenth grade, his contacts with the school and with formal education end, while the "gifted" child usually continues on through college. Sometimes the drop-out returns to school or goes to evening school, but this is not usual.

The drop-out is turning his back on education. In doing so he is telling us that we never really connected with him, that in our preoccupation with others we never gave him enough time or attention. A high-school education, in a sense, is a gift of society, though sometimes a rather costly one for the recipient. When a student refuses this gift, it indicates that something must be seriously wrong, either with the gift or with the student, and that we ought to find out what it is.

If only a few students rejected the gift, the problem would not be so alarming. But the fact is that as many students drop out of school in Big City as stay in. Of those who enter the ninth grade, it is officially claimed that 50 per cent do not remain to be graduated. The same rate holds, on an average, throughout the country. Each year about a million students in the nation drop out of school.

The 50 per cent figure appears to be only a rough estimate. Very little is known about drop-outs in Big City. Annual drop-out figures are kept on individual schools only for the senior high schools. None are kept for the elementary or junior highs, though it is known that numerous drop-outs occur at these levels—about 17.5 per cent of all the drop-outs in Big City, it is estimated.

Some drop-outs return to school or eventually enroll in

night-school classes. It is not known how many take this course or what happens to them after their return to school.

The percentage of drop-outs to total registration in each Big City senior high school during a one-year period is shown in Table 19. (The figures do not account for drop-outs in junior highs or for the fact that a very large proportion of lower-income students drop out before reaching senior high.)

TABLE 19. Percentage of Drop-outs to Total School Registration (One-Year Period)

INCOME GROUP	DROP-OUTS
1 ($5000—)	20.3%
2	23.8
3	16.9
4	21.5
5	13.9
6 ($6000—)	16.2
7	13.7
8	18.9
9 ($7000—)	12.0
10	9.1
11	6.1
12	4.5
13 ($8000—)	6.5
14	6.6
15	4.2
16	4.2
17 ($9000—)	3.6

Drop-out rates follow income levels quite closely, the lowest rate occurring in school 17, the highest in school 2. The difference between the two rates is 20.2 per cent. To state the difference another way, the drop-out rate in

school 2 is almost *six times* greater than the rate in school
17. In school 2, almost one out of every four students
dropped out of school during the course of the year.

The drop-out rates by major income groups were as follows.

INCOME GROUP	DROP-OUTS
I ($5000—)	19.2%
II ($6000—)	15.8
III ($7000—)	7.9
IV ($8000—)	7.2
V ($9000—)	3.6
A (below $7000)	17.8
B (above $7000)	6.3

About $400 is spent by Big City per year on the educa-
tion of each high-school student. During the year, 480
students dropped out of school number 2; thus a total of
$192,000 was "saved" on drop-outs in this school in one
year, an amount sufficient to pay the salaries of some
thirty extra teachers in this school. If this saving were spent
on additional teachers and various school improvements,
it would obviously make an enormous difference in the
quality of education given to the low-income students in
this school. Logically and properly this money should be
reinvested in the education of lower-income students. Such
investments might yield profitable returns in school performance and provide some measure of equal opportunity
to lower-income students.

Though much is said about the drop-out problem, very
little is known about it. Its incidence, its causes and cures
remain largely unsolved mysteries.

Former Commissioner of Education Earl McGrath puts

it this way: "Yet the truth of the matter is that, although schoolmen have many good hunches about effective ways to hold boys and girls in school, we have little valid evidence as to what will really do the job." [16]

Concerning the causes of drop-out, Richard H. Dresher says that a number of studies indicate students drop out for the following principal reasons, given in order of frequency: [17]

1. dissatisfaction with school
2. lack of personal funds
3. lure of a job
4. family support
5. inability to see relation between school subjects taken and future work
6. felt self too old for grade
7. inability to get along with teacher
8. inability to learn
9. school did not offer suitable subjects
10. illness
11. insufficient credits for graduation
12. felt self too poor in comparison with others in class
13. inability to get along with principal

Many of these reasons are closely related to social class position; perhaps all are. Except for the cover-all first response (which is too general to be meaningful), the three most frequently stated reasons for drop out directly pertain to finances: "lack of personal funds," "lure of a job," and "family support."

Reason 12 ("felt self too poor in comparison with others in class") is very intimately associated with family income levels. Perhaps this factor has a greater effect on drop-out than the position assigned it would indicate. Very often when students leave school because they feel "too poor in comparison with others in class," they and their parents are ashamed to admit it, and instead give "dissatisfaction with school" as an excuse. Robert and Helen Lynd in their famous Middletown study observed:

> A number of mothers who said that a child had left school because he "didn't like it" finally explained with great reluctance, "We couldn't dress him like we'd ought to and he felt out of it," or, "The two boys and the oldest girl all quit because they hated Central High School. They all loved the Junior High School down here, but up there they're so snobbish. If you don't dress right you haven't any friends." . . . "My oldest girl stopped because we couldn't give her no money for the right kind of clothes. The boy begged and begged to go on through high school, but his father wouldn't give him no help. Now the youngest girl has left 10B this year. She was doing just fine, but she was too proud to go to school unless she could have clothes like the other girls." [18]

Education is by no means as "free" as is commonly assumed. Dressing as others do in order to keep up socially is only one of the many costs of a high-school education. Even those who should be familiar with these costs do not have a proper estimate of them. According to Professor Harold C. Hand, high-school principals during the depression years 1931–37 estimated annual school costs to each student to be about $7.50; yet a study of these costs showed that the amount students had to spend each year to keep up socially and scholastically was actually $125.00.[19]

During these depression years about 26 per cent of all

American families had incomes of $750 a year or less, with an average (in this 26-per-cent group) of $470 a year; a family in this group therefore had to spend more than *one-fourth* of the entire family income on expenses for each child in high school. In many families, even today, the costs of a high-school education are just as prohibitive.

Some of the required and optional costs of keeping up were: admission fees for athletic contests, parties, dances, dramatic performances; dues for student body, class, or club memberships; fees or special assessments for home-making, mechanical-drawing, woodworking, laboratory-science, and other courses; charges for gym clothes, lockers, towels, domestic-science uniforms, band and orchestra instruments and uniforms, athletic equipment, rooters' caps, class sweaters, rings, keys, pins; expenditures for various tag and ribbon drives, ROTC medals, school excursions, textbooks, workbooks, pens, pencils, paper, ink; subscriptions to the school yearbook, newspaper, magazine, handbook, costs of photographs for the school yearbook and for graduation, graduation announcements, diploma fees, commencement caps and gowns.

These are simply the "in-school" costs. In addition there are burdensome out-of-school expenses such as clothes (which, as mentioned before, suddenly become the source of much social and financial concern in high school), the cost of dates, transportation by bus or car, entertaining friends or having parties at home, lunches and other meals, and other miscellaneous items.

These in-and-out-of-school expenses, when added up, are considerable enough to keep many lower-income students out of school. The mounting financial pressures in high school force many to drop out in favor of work or simply to escape from a situation where they feel "too poor in comparison with others in class."

In Big City high schools, students are required to buy their own textbooks. If a student cannot afford the costs of texts, he must apply to the school for relief; his family must then fill out a financial form, after which an investigator is sent to the home to check on family finances. Then, perhaps, texts are furnished by the schools. No provisions are made for texts in city welfare allowances, nor are provisions made by the school for students from families on relief, except on specific written request by the welfare worker.

It has been recommended by the citizens' committee that texts be furnished free to all students in the city; it is estimated that the costs would be negligible and that no initial outlay would be required, since present textbook funds (used to purchase texts for resale to students) and the costs of handling book sales would probably cover most of the costs of free texts.

Finances, to be sure, are not the only cause of drop-out; other social class factors are also very influential.

In a study of 4400 seniors in Washington State high schools, Joel B. Montague found (Table 20) that students in the Lower Social Status had many more personal, school, and social problems than other students.[20] The study was not of drop-outs, but of high-school seniors who, since they had remained in school until the twelfth grade, presumably had made a fairly successful adjustment in school. Most of the seriously troubled Lower Status students had already dropped out of school, and thus the problems of Lower Status students tended to be minimized; still, their responses suggest some explanations for the excessively high drop-out rates found in Lower Status groups.

TABLE 20. Study of Seniors in Washington State High Schools

	UPPER SOCIAL STATUS	MIDDLE SOCIAL STATUS	LOWER SOCIAL STATUS
Dissatisfaction with school			
School is not interesting	5.0%	7.0%	12.5%
Studies are too hard	1.9	1.3	6.2
Don't like my courses	3.7	4.1	9.8
Difficulties in interpersonal relations in school			
Not being popular	9.0	9.4	16.1
Being left out of things	13.5	11.0	21.4
Too few social activities	13.2	9.1	25.0
Too many social activities	8.9	4.5	1.8
How to make friends	10.8	13.9	17.9
Difficulties in self-expression in school situations			
Unable to express myself well	18.5	23.8	40.2
Don't like to recite	14.0	17.7	19.6
Self-Criticism			
Can't seem to concentrate	26.5	27.2	35.7
Not enough time to study	15.0	12.5	21.4
Afraid I'm not passing	3.1	3.8	8.0

Lower Status students are more troubled than students of higher status about every item in this table, with one exception: they do not have "too many social activities." Their most frequent complaints are that they are unable to express themselves well and that they "can't seem to concentrate."

Personal problems compounded by financial difficulties

make for trouble in school and frequent early drop-out among Lower Status students.

What's To Be Done? As mentioned before, the drop-out problem appears baffling to most schoolmen. It is our own observation, however, that schoolmen have not given the problem much serious attention. In comparison with the "gifted," at least, the drop-out is a forgotten student. Lip service is frequently given, but concern often ends there.

In Big City, though the subject is mentioned in reports, there is no specific action program aimed at drop-out *prevention,* and none seems forthcoming. In the final recommendations of the citizens' committee, the problem is mentioned in reference to junior highs, and nothing is said about senior-high drop-outs.

Neglect of the problem might be traced to at least three sources: the complex nature of the problem, the enormous savings to the schools on drop-outs, and the rather prevalent belief that students who drop out are not educable and that their leaving is "good riddance."

Whatever its source, the neglect is perhaps simply a reflection of the general neglect of the school problems of lower-income students. In a sense, solutions to the drop-out problem are dependent on solutions to other problems, drop-outs being only symptomatic of the general educational ailments of lower-income students. Of course the symptoms can and should be treated, but the ailment itself cannot be cured until basic remedies are applied.

Though Big City has no drop-out *prevention* program, it does have a *post*-drop-out program, one that is unique in the country. *Life* describes Big City's "Upgrading Program" as "the only program in the US to attack this neglected problem on any sizable scale." [21]

The program provides a brief period of job preparation and information to students who have already dropped out. The school program runs half a day for six weeks, servicing a total of two hundred students in this period.

During these six weeks students are taught that "neat hair, fresh clothing and shined shoes are necessary when applying for a job. . . . They learn that employers expect those they hire to be courteous, punctual and able to take and carry out orders. Students learn also that, in order to hold a job, they must meet the boss's requirements."

A total of ten full-time faculty members are employed in the program, and special classrooms are used in ten of the city's high schools. The program's aim is to teach good work habits, not job skills. Students come and go as they please, and no absence or tardy excuses are required. Lessons are not planned by the teacher but emerge from group discussion. The program is voluntary and open to all unemployed youths between sixteen and twenty without cost, though not all who apply are admitted.

After six weeks, many find jobs, some on referral by social agencies. About 10 per cent return to school. Those who need further aid are assigned to subsidized jobs in a city department or social agency where they work under school supervision.

The program is a good one, as far as it goes. But it barely touches the basic problem. Nothing is done to make school a more vital place for the potential drop-out nor to convince students of the value of remaining in school. Only a minor investment of school funds is made (ten full-time teachers) and only a brief six-week period of training for a relatively small number of drop-outs is offered. In sum, the program is only the *beginning* of an answer to the problem.

A cooperative work-study program has been suggested by many who are interested in drop-out, as a partial answer. Such programs offer students an opportunity to work on paying jobs while attending school, often in alternating blocks of time (two months of school, two of work).

The consensus of opinion seems to be that such programs provide excellent training for the potential drop-out. They reduce economic pressures, provide valuable experience in the world of work, and put new meaning into school studies.

Usually these programs are quite highly selective, however. Admission is not open to all students. Only those are taken who are already doing rather well in school and are rated as having good chances for success.

On the whole, the programs are few and restrictive. In Big City they are operating in only four high schools—one in a high-income school—and in three trade schools. (Trade schools, as has been noted, were not included in this study because they are not neighborhood schools but draw students from all areas of the city.)

A high-school graduate can expect to earn an average of $30,000 more, over a lifetime, than a high-school drop-out. His earnings will be $50,000 more than a person who quit in the eighth grade.

A youth without a high-school diploma is handicapped vocationally and socially. He will generally have to accept harder and lower-paying jobs. Without a skill, he may be a victim of recurrent layoff and unemployment. What is more, society has a decreasing need for his labor. Automation is eliminating thousands of unskilled jobs each year, though many skilled jobs are begging for applicants.

The problem is an acute one, both for the individual and for the nation.

The Quality of Education

Unqualified Teachers

There are not as many ESRPs (substitutes who are usually unqualified teachers) in Big City high schools as in elementary schools. The highest proportion of these unquali-

INCOME GROUP	PERCENTAGE OF ESRPS TO TOTAL TEACHING TIME
1 ($5000—)	9.8%
2	6.3
3	8.0
4	6.6
5	6.4
6 ($6000—)	3.8
7	2.5
8	1.4
9 ($7000—)	3.3
10	1.9
11	1.5
12	2.0
13 ($8000—)	1.5
14	1.4
15	1.8
16	0
17 ($9000—)	2.9

fied teachers is 9.8 per cent (in the lowest-income school); in the elementary schools the highest proportion was found to be 24 per cent. As in the early grades, the number of ESRPs in the high schools is closely related to income levels, with a few interesting variations (table, page 211).

Almost one out of every ten teachers in the lowest-income high school is an emergency substitute working on a regular assignment.

School 17 has an unexpectedly high percentage of ESRPs as compared with other high-income schools. Whether true or not it is at least *claimed* by many teachers that students in school 17 are "hard to handle"; because of this the school may have trouble holding qualified teachers and may have to accept ESRPs instead.

In the major income groups the percentage of ESRP teaching time to total teaching time is:

INCOME GROUP	PERCENTAGE OF ESRPS TO TOTAL TEACHING TIME
I ($5000—)	7.4%
II ($6000—)	2.6
III ($7000—)	2.2
IV ($8000—)	1.5
V ($9000—)	2.9
A (below $7000)	5.6
B (above $7000)	2.0

Thus the percentage of ESRPs in the lower-income half is almost three times greater than the percentage in the upper-income half.

Class Size

Class size is only a fraction larger in the lower-income half than in the upper half, with an average size in group A of 33.6 and in group B of 33.3. The distribution among major income groups is:

INCOME GROUP	CLASS SIZE
I ($5000—)	33.2
II ($6000—)	34.3
III ($7000—)	33.6
IV ($8000—)	32.6
V ($9000—)	34.8

The largest class size, by a small fraction of 1 per cent, is found in group V, which is contrary to what might have been expected.

Continuous Class Programs and Overcrowding

A student with a continuous class program is one whose high school is so crowded and whose program is so compact that he must go to classes without any breaks except a lunch period. These continuous programs have been under hot attack in Big City recently, and a clamor has risen to relieve congestion in certain schools so that students can have more free periods.

Certainly continuous programs do not provide the best possible educational situation, since they do not allow time for relaxation and study between classes. Students with continuous programs, however, are not disadvantaged *educationally;* they take as many classes as they can handle, and they are as free as other students to take classes of their own choice. Frequently students *prefer* continuous programs because of the shortened school day.

The protests, it would therefore appear, may be somewhat out of proportion to the size of the problem, especially since there is so little public clamor for correction of other school problems—delinquency, failure, dreary curriculums, unqualified teachers, school buildings unfit for use, totally inadequate health and psychological services, etc. Nor has there been much clamor about over-crowding at the elementary school level, perhaps because crowding at this level is more common in lower-income areas, while high-school crowding is found mostly in upper-income areas. In elementary schools overcrowding is dealt with by transporting students to other schools; the high-school problem could also be handled this way except that upper-income students might object to being sent to the less crowded lower-income schools. Table 21 shows that overcrowding and continuous class programs are more common in upper-income areas.

TABLE 21. Continuous Class Programs

INCOME GROUP	NUMBER OF SCHOOLS IN EACH INCOME GROUP	NUMBER OF SCHOOLS WITH CONTINUOUS PROGRAMS
I ($5000—)	5	0
II ($6000—)	3	1
III ($7000—)	4	1
IV ($8000—)	4	3
V ($9000—)	1	1
A (below $7000)	8	1
B (above $7000)	9	5

Thus more than half the schools in the upper-income half have continuous class programs; in the lower-income half only one school out of eight has a continuous program. In this aspect of school life, lower-income groups appear to be receiving better school service than upper-income groups.

School Buildings

High-school buildings in the lower-income half are more than twice as old as buildings in the upper-income half. Except for the reversed positions of groups III and IV, the age of school buildings tends to decrease as income increases. Schools in group I are more than four times as old as in group V.

INCOME GROUP	AVERAGE AGE OF BUILDINGS
I ($5000—)	45.0
II ($6000—)	38.0
III ($7000—)	18.5
IV ($8000—)	24.5
V ($9000—)	10.0
A (below $7000)	42.5
B (above $7000)	20.2

Most high schools in Big City are cramped for outdoor recreational space, some more than others. The most serious shortage of outdoor space is found in the lower-income areas, where homes and neighborhoods tend to be overcrowded, parks and recreation areas in short supply, and delinquency rates unusually high. Unexpectedly, group III has the most adequate acreage.

The first table on page 216 indicates the percentage of acreage increase needed to provide proper outdoor space for the pupils and staff housed in the school buildings.

Schools in the lower-income half need almost twice as great an acreage increase as schools in the upper-income half, and schools in group I need an 86-per-cent acreage increase.

The almost total inadequacy of outdoor school space in

group I, in addition to the shortage of park and recreation space, raises the serious question: Where do students in these lowest-income schools find space for healthy outdoor recreation? They live in crowded homes with little yard space; there are almost no vacant lots in their downtown neighborhoods, and they cannot play in the streets because of heavy traffic. They seldom go to parks outside their neighborhoods, and they almost never go camping or hiking. Where do they play?

INCOME GROUP	PERCENTAGE OF ACREAGE INCREASE NEEDED *
I ($5000—)	86%
II ($6000—)	66
III ($7000—)	35
IV ($8000—)	43
V ($9000—)	47
A (above $7000)	78
B (below $7000)	40

* Schools with acreage used by adjacent elementary and junior highs were not included here.

Facilities in the highest-income high school are much better than in the lowest-income school, as Table 22 shows.

By major income groups the average number of "Lacking or sub-standard" facilities per school is as follows.

INCOME GROUP	LACKING OR SUB-STANDARD FACILITIES
I ($5000—)	23
II ($6000—)	19
III ($7000—)	14
IV ($8000—)	17
V ($9000—)	11

Except for the reversals of groups III and IV, facilities tend to improve as income increases.

TABLE 22. Lacking or Sub-Standard Facilities *

	SCHOOL 1 (LOWEST INCOME)	SCHOOL 17 (HIGHEST INCOME)
Counselors' offices	o	x
Auditorium workroom	o	x
Choral music room	S	x
Orchestral music room	S	x
Music practice room	o	x
Electrical shop	o	x
Shop lecture room	o	x
Arts and crafts	o	x
Home living	o	x
Library workroom	o	x
Orthopedic room	o	x
Clinic	o	x
Retailing	o	x
ROTC classroom	o	x
Student publication room	o	x
Age of building	44	10

KEY

o = lacking
S = sub-standard
x = facility present and in good condition

* Those facilities which were found to be lacking or sub-standard in *both* schools are not included in this list; only the differences are included.

The citizens' report on school buildings, the most painstaking and thorough in the city's history, has been discussed previously in reference to elementary-school buildings. It need only be repeated that this committee visited all schools in the city, studied all aspects of the school plant, and gave separate ratings to every building detail examined. The ten major categories of the study were: adequacy, suitability, safety, healthfulness, accessibility, flexibility, efficiency, economy, expansibility, and appearance. The highest possible score in each of these ten categories was 100. A "perfect" score in all ten categories would therefore be 1000. Total building scores of each high school are shown in Table 23.

TABLE 23. Total Building Scores (perfect score: 1000) *

1. ($5000—)	575—
2.	706
3.	501—
4.	641—
5.	761
6. ($6000—)	661—
7.	+888
8.	606—
9. ($7000—)	+816
10.	+948
11.	788
12.	+841
13. ($8000—)	792
14.	717
15.	+833
16.	+879
17. ($9000—)	+893

* A plus indicates a rating of over 800; a minus of under 700.

Thus five high schools in the lower-income half (below $7000) received scores of less than 700, and only one school had a rating of over 800.

In the upper-income half, there were no schools scoring

below 700, and there were six (out of nine) scoring over 800.

Scores of the major income groups were as follows.

INCOME GROUP	BUILDING SCORE
I ($5000—)	637
II ($6000—)	718
III ($7000—)	848
IV ($8000—)	805
V ($9000—)	893
A (below $7000)	667
B (above $7000)	834

Again, except for the reversed positions of groups III and IV, the quality of school buildings and facilities tends to improve as income increases.

A very substantial difference in the scores of groups A and B will be noticed, a difference amounting to 167 points.

Among the *individual* schools the difference between the lowest- and the highest-income schools is 318 points!

Table 24 gives these scores some concrete meaning by pointing out specific factors contributing to the superiority of upper-income high schools. The comparison is made between the lowest and the highest major income groups (groups I and V).

In all items listed, building scores are higher, often much higher, in the upper-income group.

According to a citizens' committee report, "schools serving the wealthy areas of the city frequently receive gifts of equipment either from parent organizations or from individual citizens." Such facilities include radios, television

TABLE 24. Breakdown of Building Scores (numbers in parentheses indicate the "perfect" score)

	SCORES	
	GROUP I	GROUP V
Adequacy		
Play areas (5)	1.2	5.0
Size of classrooms (10)	6.6	8.0
Equipment classrooms (5)	4.4	5.0
Enough chalk boards (2)	1.4	3.0
Suitability		
Art (5)	3.6	5.0
Music (5)	2.4	5.0
Business (5)	3.8	5.0
Library (5)	4.4	5.0
Assembly (2)	1.2	2.0
Hot lunches (3)	2.0	3.0
Homemaking (5)	4.2	5.0
Shop work (5)	2.8	5.0
Audio-visual equipment (5)	3.6	5.0
Outdoor site suitably equipped and developed (5)	.6	3.0
Safety		
Stairway safe (5)	3.8	5.0
Fire control facilities (5)	4.0	5.0
Hazards walks & drives (5)	2.8	5.0
Equipment hazards (5)	0	5.0
Separate play areas (5)	1.0	5.0
Healthfulness		
Proper lighting (15)	10.4	15.0
Seats proper size (10)	6.4	10.0
Heating & ventilation satisfactory (10)	7.6	10.0
Toilet facilities adequate (10)	6.6	10.0
Flexibility		
Multiple use of rooms (10)	4.2	10.0
Furniture movable (10)	2.6	8.0

sets, tape recorders, records, phonographs, mimeographs
and office machines, etc. Since these facilities have never
been inventoried, it is suggested that a tabulation be made
of them with a view to equalization.

Many of these facilities are essential to school operation
and should be provided for by the school budget rather
than by voluntary contributions or "special" funds. To
illustrate, the author recently spent some time in two Big
City high schools, one the lowest-income school and the
other among the highest. In the lowest-income high school
there was only one ditto machine available for teacher
use, and no mimeograph machine or other office equipment. The ditto machine was rarely used, since teachers
were required to buy their own paper and ditto stencils,
costly items when a teacher has some 175 students who
need materials. In addition, since no office staff was provided, it was necessary for teachers to type their own stencils and run off their own ditto copies. Needless to say,
this was seldom done.

In the upper-income school an unlimited quantity of
paper and stencils was available to teachers, without
charge. The funds for these supplies had been raised
through special student-parent activities. Office services
were also available, saving teachers the trying and time-
consuming job of typing and duplicating their own material, (a job which teachers without typing and office
skills could not perform at all). Yet duplicated materials,
prepared by the teacher (tests, assignments, bibliographies,
charts, tables, text supplements, etc.) are essential to high-
quality education, and should be provided for by the
schools and not by special funds.

Such inequalities in basic educational tools are common-place in the schools of Big City.

Which Income Group is Worst Off?

In most aspects of school life, the lowest major income group (group I) appears to be much worse off than any of the other groups. However, group II (the second-lowest income group) appears to be worse off in the following ways.

In the elementary schools, class size was largest in group II (30.9 as compared with 29.7 in group I).

There were more unqualified teachers (19.1 per cent as compared with 13.9 per cent in group I).

The average age of buildings was somewhat higher (46 years as compared with 45 years in group I). Total building scores in group II, however, were slightly higher than in group I (578.3 as compared with 573.5).

Only the lowest-income families can qualify for admission as tenants in Big City's public housing developments, on the sites of which new school buildings have been erected. Because children living in these developments go to the newly constructed schools on the site, they have available to them facilities often equal to those provided in the highest-income areas. Children of the lowest-income group who do not live at these sites, however, are housed in the city's oldest and most inadequate buildings.

Parent membership in elementary-school groups was slightly higher in group II (12.3 per 100 students, as compared with 10.1 in group I), although some of the very lowest levels of parent participation were found in group II—in the $6000 income range.

In high school, summer-school enrollment was lowest in group II. On the other hand, in high school, there were more unqualified teachers and school buildings were older and considerably more inadequate in group I, the lowest-income group.

It appears, therefore, that in some important respects, particularly in the elementary schools, group II is somewhat worse off than group I. It should not be assumed, then, that the very lowest income groups are *always* at the bottom of the educational ladder.

In almost all aspects of school life, the greatest differences have been between schools under $7000 income and those over $7000. The great divide separating these two groups is apparent in the number of "gifted" children chosen, the number of parents active in school affairs, school buildings and facilities, the per cent of unqualified teachers, etc.

Thus the line of greatest separation seems to coincide almost exactly with the average family income level— which in Big City is $6900 a year.

5

Control of the Schools

Action is the line of the greatest resistance . . .
The most characteristically and peculiarly moral judgments
that a man is ever called on to make are in unprecedented
cases and lonely emergencies where no popular rhetorical
maxim can avail, and the hidden oracle alone can speak;
and it speaks often in favor of conduct quite unusual and
suicidal as far as gaining popular approbation goes.
—William James, *Principles of Psychology*

CONTROL OF THE SCHOOLS

Before final comments and suggestions, one last matter should be discussed—control of the schools. It is no small matter; in fact, it explains a great deal about why schools are what they are—reflections of the social class system in the outside world, and in some sense the creators and guardians of this system.

Schools are "controlled" by school boards (and their administrators). Though these boards are the ultimate decision-makers, they are much influenced by two other groups—teachers and parents.

Parents

Our tabulations showed that for every 100 students there were 73.8 parents who belonged to elementary-school parent organizations in group IV (the highest-income group), as compared with only 10.1 in group I.

At the very highest income level (minor group 26) there were more individual parent members than there were students in school. The lowest parent membership was 3.8 (per 100 students) in one of the lower-income groups (group 6).

So it is that parents in upper-income groups have close contact with the schools through parent organizations, while those in lower-income groups usually have no contact at all.

Furthermore, upper-income parents frequently consult with teachers, counselors, the school principal, the super-intendent, and even school-board members about their children and school affairs. Lower-income parents seldom talk with any of these people. When an upper-income parent has a grievance, he talks to the appropriate person at school about it; he talks this person's language and he regards himself as at least an equal; he is usually educated, articulate, and impressive, a person to be respected and reckoned with. Whatever the complaint is about—marks, curriculum, teachers, etc.—chances are it will be given serious attention.

But lower-income parents, either individually or in groups, have little effect on the school's operations. They seldom seek out contact with the school, since they usually do not have enough confidence or "know how" for this. The criticisms they have of the schools are often unformed and ill-defined. They are not articulate or well educated; they are self conscious about themselves and the way they dress, and they generally feel uncomfortable and out of place in school. What is more, they are often afraid of the teachers and principals and therefore timid about raising complaints with them. Because of these things, lower-income parents seldom visit the school or attend "open house" ceremonies, even when they are seriously worried about their children. Almost never would they think of calling the principal, the superintendent, or a board member about their complaints, and it would be almost unheard of for them to act as a group in making such complaints. Needless to say, they almost never meet any of these people socially, as upper-income groups do—a subtle and powerful means of influencing people.

In brief, almost all the parental pressures on the schools come from upper-income groups, pressures which are often reflected in the top-ranking priority given by the schools to the problems of upper-income students, and in the general neglect of the problems of lower-income students. Some lower-income groups are now becoming more active and aggressive in their relations with the schools in Big City, and perhaps this will help to correct some of the present imbalances.

Teachers

Because of their numbers and their influence in the classroom, teachers play a significant role in school decision-making.

In the past teachers have come in overwhelming proportions from middle- and upper-income groups. Recent studies show they are now coming more and more from lower-income groups, though the proportion from unskilled laboring families is still *far* below the proportion of such workers in the population.

What is more behavior-determining than class *origin,* however, is the class *orientation* of teachers. Here the evidence is that teachers, in certain vital matters, have a class outlook very similar to that of upper-income groups and quite unlike that of "urban labor" groups.

As an example of this class outlook, V. M. Sims has found that there is a strongly conservative bias among teachers. A comparison of teachers' attitudes with those of other occupational groups reveals that teachers are 71 per cent "conservative," while urban labor is only 29 per cent "conservative." At the other political and personality extreme, only 4 per cent of teachers were found to have "radical" attitudes, while 38 per cent of urban labor fitted this category, as the figures in Table 25 show.[1]

TABLE 25. Classification of Attitudes of Occupational Groups

OCCUPATIONAL GROUP	CONSERVATIVE	INTERMEDIATE	RADICAL
Teachers	71%	25%	4%
All urban business, professional, and white-collar groups, combined	68	21	11
Large business owners	87	11	2
Professional	70	19	11
White-collar	56	28	16
Urban labor	29	33	38

What does this conservatism have to do with the kind of treatment given students in school? Sometimes, nothing; usually, a great deal. In this author's experience, teachers with a conservative bias are not likely to recognize the claims of lower-income groups to equal educational opportunity; they are not likely to recognize their need for special treatment; they are much less likely to understand lower-income students and much more likely to take offense at their behavior and to favor students from upper-income groups.

Of course there are numbers of teachers, even among those in the conservative category, who are extremely generous in their relations with lower-income children (especially when these children "behave themselves"). This is particularly true, according to reports, in some of the very lowest-income schools. In these schools there is usually found a number of devoted teachers who work there because they like the children and want very much to help them. But with a great many teachers, if not a majority, there seems to be a deficiency of the understanding and insight needed to solve the educational problems of lower-income students. And there is a distinct lack, among almost everyone connected with the schools, of the kind of reformist zeal necessary to change the present situation in the schools to any appreciable degree.

It has often been observed, in confirmation of these figures, that teachers tend to identify with upper-income groups—with their opinions, aspirations, and way of life—and many of them long to be accepted in this stratum. If the longing is great enough and the identification strong, there will be little room left for the problems of their poorer charges, little sympathy, little understanding, and little real desire to help.

Instead there may be indifference—and, at worst, contempt—for the children who violate the codes they cherish. Where possible, there may be escape into more "refined" settings.

Professor Handlin describes the teacher of the immigrant child, an earlier but not vanished breed.

Perhaps a few were touched with sympathy at the condition of their charges. But what these offered was pity, nobler than contempt, but to the children no more acceptable. It was rare indeed to find the dedicated woman whose understanding of her students brought a touch of love into her work.

After all, it was not of this they had dreamed in normal school when they had surrendered a part of their girlhood to acquire a profession, that they would devote the rest of their lives to the surveillance of a pack of unwashed ruffians.

Mostly the teachers kept their distance, kept flickering the hope that a transfer might take them to a nicer district with nicer pupils from nicer homes. When that hope died, bitterness was born; and there was thereafter more savagery than love in their instruction. To admit the least question of the rightness of what they taught would undermine the whole structure of their self-esteem. So a boy should look and be, so a home, and so a parent.[2]

Teachers are by no means the only ones who prefer association with their equals and superiors. Perhaps this is simply normal and human. Perhaps *most* people prefer associations with privileged groups—some more than others. Dedicated reformers, after all, are extremely rare. It is difficult to find people who will happily, willingly, and by preference work in areas where crime, disease, and illiteracy levels are high, and where children often come to school dirty, sullen, violent, and disobedient. The work is trying in such areas and often very discouraging. Many teachers who work with these problems grow to dislike their work and—even worse—their students. When a chance presents itself, they transfer to "better" schools.

Perhaps this is simply a human reaction, shared by all. If so, it should not be too severely criticized. What *should* be criticized is that often a teacher with the reformer's zeal needed for successful work in lower-income areas is unwelcome in the schools. If he is well bred, well dressed, and well behaved, of course, he will have a better chance for acceptance or at least toleration.

Unfortunately, reformers are often eccentric in their habits. They are not always well mannered, well dressed, and well behaved, much less likable. They disagree, they argue, and they are active rather than passive in temperament. They want to change things. They are not always pleasant with their superiors. Often, with their colleagues, they are not "one of the boys."

But, offensive as their behavior may sometimes be, reformers are rather desperately needed. The schools, therefore, should not only make a place for them, but should actively seek them out and encourage them to teach, however troublesome they may prove to be.

The welcome mat is not always out. To illustrate: A Critic Teacher in a Big City high school recently told the author that she intended to fail one of her student teachers (a university student) because, among other things, the boy was a "social reformer." Social-studies teachers, she claimed, should not be reformers because reformers are not "objective."

She said further that the teacher's job was to teach students about "how great America is." Good teachers, she said, should not raise such matters as "how we took land from the Indians when we came here" or suggest that "Columbus did not really discover America." Such ideas, according to her view, only lead to doubt and confusion, and while questions are all right after students have a "firm foundation in Americanism," they are dangerous before. Since only one class in this period of American history was offered students in this school, they presumably were never to get beyond this "firm foundation" into the question period.

The attitude of this Critic Teacher seems rather typical of the reception given in the schools to "reformist" ideas. Yet the situation seems to require that the schools extend themselves to find and hire people who are aggressive, active and passionate in their desire to raise the educational and living standards of lower-income groups.

School Boards

School boards are at the very top of the educational totem pole. They exercise the final authority on school matters. They hire the school superintendent who, in turn, hires teachers and administrative staff. Because of this power to hire and fire and make policy, the whole school system —teachers, students, administrators, curriculum—tends to be modeled after the general character and quality of the school board.

A number of studies have shown that school-board members come in overwhelming proportions from upper-income groups and are engaged mostly in business and professional occupations.

The seven members of the Big City school board are engaged in the following occupations:

2—housewives
1—advertising executive

1—executive of one of the largest corporations in Big City
1—owner of a steel company
1—owner of medium-sized business
1—physician (Negro)

Although Big City is very highly unionized, there are no representatives of organized labor on the board of education. This is not to say that there is no one on the board who is sympathetic to labor; some are, either more or less. Most of the members have even received labor endorsement during elections. However, since labor has often felt it necessary to endorse only candidates presumed to be highly electable, its endorsement is by no means an indication of wholehearted approval. In general the relations between the school board and administrative officials on the one hand and organized labor on the other have not been very close or warm, and some board members elected with labor endorsement have moved in a conservative direction in order to disassociate themselves from the "stigma" of labor support.

Only in recent years have minority ethnic groups won representation on the board. In Big City's history only one Irish Catholic, one Jew, and one Negro have served on the board. No person with an identifiably Italian or Polish name has ever been elected. Yet, taken together, these "minority" groups represent a majority of Big City's population.

Upper-income groups tend to dominate school boards in other areas of the country too. Roy W. Caughran found, for example, that school boards in the state of Illinois in 1956 tended to be selected from "upper" and "upper-middle" class groups and that, while farm representation on the Illinois boards had decreased, the businessmen's representation had increased.[3]

According to Robert Havighurst, a number of studies have shown that about 75 per cent of all board members are business proprietors, business managers, professional workers, or wives of such men, and that from 3 per cent to 15 per cent are manual workers.[4]

The authors of *Democracy in Jonesville* note that in Jonesville "the members of the Board of Education come from the two upper classes and have to qualify under three strictly administered ground rules: first, only men are eligible; second, Catholics, Jews, Irish and Democrats are informally disqualified; and third, the Board is 'non-political.' To become a member of the Board a man has to be a Protestant, a Republican, a property owner, and a Rotarian or, at the very least, approved by the Rotarians." [5]

Upper-income business and professional groups dominate school boards for a number of reasons, among them the following.

Membership on school boards is generally a non-paying job, and board meetings are often held during working hours. Thus only people who can afford, and are able, to miss time from work or who are unemployed (as housewives) can afford to serve on school boards.

Election campaigns, especially in a big city, cost a great deal of money. Only upper-income groups can afford these expenses without substantial aid from organized groups. Sometimes labor unions support candidates, but labor is almost the only group representing the interests of people with low and moderate incomes that participates in school-board elections.

School boards generally are "nonpartisan." Oddly enough, it usually turns out in "nonpartisan" elections that conservatives get elected to office in disproportionately large numbers.

In Big City, elections for the school board are "special" elections, that is, they are held in the spring, when other public offices are not in contest. Only a very small minority of the electorate—generally less than 10 per cent—participates. Not surprisingly, this electorate is relatively conservative.

Lower-income individuals and organizations have not shown much interest in school-board elections, regarding them often as of rather minor importance compared with "political" elections. This is probably directly attributable to the generally unsatisfactory experiences lower-income groups have had in school, and to the sense of alienation that has resulted from these experiences.

It is true that organized labor has played an increasingly active part in school elections, but it has tended to support non-labor and sometimes even rather conservative candidates in the perhaps mistaken belief that avowedly labor candidates cannot be elected.

Since school boards have the ultimate authority in school affairs, and since school systems tend to be cast in their image, it would seem that the first step in a program to improve education for lower-income children would be to elect board members who are aggressively interested in the problems of underprivileged groups.

A Fourth Force

Newspapers have exercised a powerful influence on the schools in Big City. They endorse board candidates and often control the decisions of school administrators and board members through publicity and the threat of "exposure." Reporters from the papers sit at every board meeting, while other organizations are seldom represented. Frequently they influence school personnel by the simple device of criticizing them by name in their columns. For example, several times recently one of the daily newspapers in Big City has editorially criticized a board member who raised questions about equality of educational offerings in the city's schools. The criticism was sharp and personal and, since the editorial was unsigned, there was no opportunity for personal counter-attack, even if there had been a desire on the part of this board member to make one. Fortunately this board member did not backtrack or capitulate under this attack. Ordinarily school personnel seem unusually sensitive to this kind of public censure, sometimes reversing position in order to accommodate school practices to press demands.

The daily papers in Big City are politically conservative. In public statements of educational policy, in their attitudes toward underprivileged children, delinquency, money expenditure, taxes, education of the "gifted," they speak almost exclusively for upper-income groups. And school administrators have seemed to be noticeably quick to follow their lead.

6

Up to Date

The harvest truly is great but the laborers are few:
pray ye therefore the lord of the harvest, that he
would send forth laborers into his harvest.

Luke 10:2

UP TO DATE

Big City

The facts and the problems described here continue in Big City. In very recent months, however, there appears to have been some slightly perceptible forward movement in the solution of these problems.

A citizens' committee on school equality has been set up and will examine for a one-year period the quality of education offered in various areas of Big City. The committee is modeled after a similar committee in New York City, except that, unlike the New York committee, it will not focus its study exclusively on racial inequalities.

Also in recent months, a small group of segregationists lost decisively in a struggle to prevent the transportation by bus of children from overcrowded elementary schools in low-income areas (many of them Negro) to under-utilized schools in predominantly white neighborhoods.

Though some parents in the all-white area protested, paraded, threatened to keep their children home and recall the members of the board of education, the decision was held firmly and the few disgruntled parents quickly gave in. Some of the parents have simply shifted their tactics of opposition, but the fact remains that their children now attend integrated schools without incident or disturbance.

This year, with a $135,900 foundation grant and match-ing funds from the board of education, an experimental program was undertaken in seven schools in culturally de-pressed areas of the city. The emphasis of the program is on community work, raising the aspiration levels of parents and children, providing remedial reading help to students, and in-service training of teachers.

The program is small but it is at least a beginning.

New York City

New York City appears to be far ahead of all other areas in the attention given to problems raised here. The atten-tion, in this case, has been focused mainly on minority-group problems. Apparently New York was more im-pressed than other cities with the serious implications of the Supreme Court decision on Southern schools, and with the growing desire of minority groups for expanding op-portunities.

The turning point in New York was a speech made in 1954 by Dr. Kenneth B. Clark, an important contributor to the Supreme Court decision, on the subject of Northern

school segregation. In this speech he said: "As I understand the decision, the US Supreme Court has clearly stated
that segregation itself damages the personality of human
beings. . . . Northern schools are bound to put their own
houses in order, if they are to obey the spirit of this
decision."

The next day the president of the board of education
called for a full-scale inquiry into the status of Negro and
Puerto Rican children in New York City schools.

The inquiry uncovered marked inequalities in education provided these groups, with inferior facilities and less
qualified teachers being found in minority-group schools.
As a result of the study, the schools attempted (often under
continuing pressure) to do two things:

1. Make alterations in the quite rigid pattern of segregation in New York schools. This year, for the first time,
minority-group students from segregated schools were
permitted to register in schools outside their own districts.
Though a landslide of transfer requests was expected
(3000 was the estimate), only about 600 students out of
about 18,000 eligible to transfer made requests, and even
fewer went through with the change. The integrated
schools are now operating without even minor disturbance.
Many believed, with Kenneth B. Clark, that integration
would raise the educational levels of whites as well as of
Negroes. Clark wrote in the *Teachers College Record:*

> Segregated education is inferior and nonadaptive for
> whites as well as Negroes. Put simply, no child can receive
> a democratic education in a non-democratic school.
>
> A racially segregated school imposes upon white children
> the inevitable stultifying burdens of petty provincialism,
> irrational fears and hatreds of people who are different,

and a distorted image of themselves. Psychologically the racially segregated school at this period of American and world history is an anachronism which our nation can not afford. This point must be made over and over again until it is understood by those who have the power to make the decisions which control our destiny.[1]

2. Compensate for the inferior quality of education offered in many minority-group schools. To accomplish this, several major projects have been undertaken. The most important are the Higher Horizons Project and a program of concentrated attention to educational standards in "Special Service" schools.

The Higher Horizons Project tries to raise the aspirations of culturally deprived children. It focuses not on the "gifted" but on *all* the children at specified grade levels in depressed-area schools. Its limitations are its size and budget. Out of a total New York City public-school population of about *one million,* only 32,000 students are involved in the program.

The cost is 15 cents per child per day, or $27 a year. The whole cost is met by the board of education, without foundation aid.

The program began operation in February of 1959. Out of a total annual public-school budget in New York City of $400,000,000, the total yearly cost of Higher Horizons will be about $685,000. This can be compared with the $40,000,000 in "operating" budget alone which New York spends each year on its free colleges. Little of this free-college money, it appears, reaches students from depressed-area schools, though in former years this was apparently not the case.

The program in Special Service schools is also a new creation, designed to equalize facilities, teaching staff, and educational opportunities in minority-group areas. There are now 150 of these schools out of a total of 840 New York public schools.

In these schools, the emphasis has been on reducing class size, providing additional counseling services and lunch-room aides, and reducing the number of unqualified teachers.

Perhaps the biggest gain in the program has been in reducing class size. Still, the difference is small. In the Special Service elementary school, there are now 27.8 pupils per class. In all elementary schools, the average is 29.7. (*Actual* class size, excluding non-teaching personnel from the calculations, is larger in both cases.)

The program's goals are certainly commendable. Its administration at top levels appears to be quite energetic and imaginative. Yet its operations—given its limited budget, the inertia of some school principals, and the lack of parental pressure—fall far short of the need and the demand for educational services in depressed areas.

Though advanced in *some* respects, New York City schools are, in other respects, less democratic than Big City schools. The New York City system, for example, does not have a *single truly comprehensive high school* of the type acclaimed by James B. Conant.

Instead, most of the city's 85 high schools offer either academic or vocational programs (29 vocational and 56 academic).

The Great Cities Project

Until very recent months, no city other than New York has given much more than passing verbal attention to the problems of low-income, culturally deprived students. Their problems, however, cannot be ignored for long. It is estimated that one out of every *three* children in city schools now falls into the category of the culturally deprived—as compared with one out of *ten* in 1950.

The only effort that seems to deserve special note here is the Great Cities project. This program has provided about $100,000 of Ford Foundation funds to each of seven cities (Chicago, Philadelphia, Detroit, St. Louis, Pittsburgh, Cleveland, Milwaukee) for a one-year period, 1960–61.

Strangely and unfortunately, though the New York City Higher Horizons project served as a model and an inspiration for the Great Cities project, the city of New York was completely by-passed in the awarding of funds. Thus the one city in the nation that had demonstrated interest, competence, and good intention was apparently penalized for efforts it had undertaken on its own in behalf of the culturally deprived child.

The emphasis of the Great Cities project is on raising aspiration levels of both parents and students, though each city is free to work out its own program. In some cases the funds are being matched by local money. In Philadelphia, in addition to the project schools, the city is operating with its own funds an experimental program in one of its depressed-area high schools. On the West Coast there is some discussion but almost no activity.

Britain

The problems explored here seem to be the same the whole world over. In other areas of the world they are even more serious than they are here.

British schools, for example, are more rigid than American schools in their pattern of class segregation and offer even fewer opportunities to lower-income students.

In Britain the children of professional and managerial parents can expect, in the *majority* of cases, to stay in school full-time until age seventeen. The children of unskilled workers have about one chance in ten of staying on. Yet the sons of manual workers make up about 40 per cent of the top "ability" group, as judged by an Army survey.

At age *eleven*, students are required to take comprehensive examinations that will determine the type of secondary school they will enter: grammar school (an academic college-prep school), or the Secondary Modern school, which offers a more general and vocational curriculum. The decision is compulsory and virtually irrevocable.

In many schools, including the majority of Secondary Moderns, no courses are offered to students staying in school beyond age fifteen. Result: of the 11,482 children who left school in 1958 to go to a university, only 13 came from Secondary Modern schools.

Some 70 per cent of all students in state-maintained schools are in Secondary Moderns. Observers note that the present system is a segregated one. The Secondary Modern schools are almost entirely working-class, and the grammar schools are quite exclusively middle-class.

English secondary schools are not "comprehensive," as most American high schools are, housing under one roof a wide range of students and subjects—the academic as well as the vocational. Also, a very large percentage of higher-income families send their children to private schools, where they are prepared, even in very early and tender years, for college entrance.

The boldest suggestions for school reform in England have come from some individuals in the Labour party and trade unions. One proposal is that the private schools be abolished. Another is that the age of decision be raised from eleven to a somewhat more mature age. (Research shows that a postponement till age fifteen would have changed the educational fate of 14 per cent of all students; a higher estimate claims 29 per cent.)

Still another proposal is that the separate schools (grammar and Secondary Modern) be combined into one comprehensive school.

The recent Crowther report recommends that the minimum school leaving age be raised to sixteen by 1969. The timetable, apparently, is being ignored.

About 100,000 students are now working for a bachelor's degree in British colleges and universities. In France and West Germany, with roughly similar total populations, enrollments are 240,000 and 200,000, respectively. The Philippines, with a population of 23 million (less than half of Britain), has over 350,000 students working for a college degree.

Seymour Martin Lipset, Professor of Sociology at the University of California, comments:

The important expansion of English universities which has occurred since 1945 is just the beginning of what would be needed to democratize English intellectual and political life, to reduce the monopoly which those who have attended the ancient universities have on the key positions within the society. . . .

There are few institutions in British life which strike an American as more indicative of the continuing strength of elitist values in British culture than its educational system. At least to me, this is a system based on the premise that a nation needs only a small highly educated elite, and that the vast majority need only that modicum of education which gives them elementary literacy and the skills necessary to operate industry and to occupy the lower rungs of white-collar employment.[2]

"It may even be argued," Lipset observes, "that the power of the elite in Britain is supported more through its monopoly of good education than by any other source."

7

Comments and Suggestions

I think by far the most important bill in our whole code is that for diffusion of knowledge among the people. No surer foundation can be devised for the preservation of peace and happiness. . . .
Preach a crusade against ignorance; establish and improve the law for educating the common people . . . the people alone can protect us against the evils [of misgovernment].
—Thomas Jefferson

COMMENTS AND SUGGESTIONS

Finances

A great deal more money is now being spent by the schools of Big City in upper-income areas. Certainly an argument can be made that in a democratic society the reverse of this should be true, since need is greater in lower-income areas. Present inequalities in school expenditures are:

Drop-Outs: In one low-income high school alone, $192,-000 was saved in one year on drop-outs. Education for lower-income students is therefore costing much less than the education of upper-income students, who rarely drop out of school before graduation.

Buildings and facilities: It is obvious from our data that a great deal more money has been spent for school buildings and facilities in upper-income areas.

Teachers: Considerably more money is being spent on teachers' salaries in upper-income schools, since ESRPs and inexperienced teachers, who are heavily concentrated in low-income areas, are paid less in wages and fringe benefits than regular experienced teachers.

Club Activities: Indications are that most of the advantages of club activities go to upper-income students. These activities take up a great deal of teacher time and are therefore costly.

"Gifted"-Child Programs: These costly programs service upper-income students almost exclusively.

Evening School, Summer School, Parent Groups, Adult Activities: Since these services are provided disproportionately to upper-income groups, whatever costs are involved, in either teacher time or more direct expenditures, are being unequally distributed.

Another Related Cost Item: Each year about $3.6 billion is spent on higher education at the college and university level; this amounts to about one dollar for every four and a half spent on public-school education. Most of this money comes from public subsidies, though seldom from local board-of-education funds. *Most of this $3.6 billion is being spent on upper-income students, who make up the bulk of the college population.*

Possible reverse inequalities are:

Attendance Officers: Because Attendance Department areas did not coincide in any manageable way with our area divisions, the distribution of these services could not be determined. The main function of the Attendance Department, however, is law enforcement, a police rather than a social-service function.

Visiting Teachers: Since the department in charge of the Visiting Teacher program would not release any information, nothing could be determined about the distribution of these services.

Detention School: Detention School and Ungraded classrooms cost more to operate than regular classrooms, and lower-income children receive more "services" from these programs than upper-income children. However, if other educational costs were equitably distributed and counseling, Visiting Teacher, and other services were apportioned according to need, perhaps Detention School services, as well as Attendance Department services, would correspondingly decrease. It could also be expected that, with adequate educational and guidance services for low-income groups, the public costs of crime, prisons, mental institutions, and public-assistance programs would perhaps also tend to diminish.

We suggest, therefore, as a first step in providing equal educational opportunity to all children, that school expenditures be equalized, at the very least, among the various income groups. It may not be possible, or even desirable, to attempt an exact equalization of *facilities*, but it should be possible, as it would be highly desirable, to equalize *expenditures*.

Federal aid to education and other school-finance proposals are not at issue here. High-quality education, however, for whatever income group, costs money, more of it than we do or can raise by present school taxes.

Federal assistance is an obvious and pressing educational need—not so much in Big City as in areas where high-quality schools cannot be supported locally. Yet Big City is directly concerned with schools in other areas, for their products often end up Big City schools.

In these stateside-underdeveloped areas the children most likely to be short-changed are lower-income children, the same ones who seem to pull the short straw everywhere in the country. In this case, however, the deprivation is acute and desperate.

Big City schools too need more money to operate on, much more. Major reforms can hardly be undertaken without money and lots of it. Those concerned about our national destiny should be willing to pay. Nowhere is money more securely invested than in our schools, and nowhere are the returns greater, to upper-, lower-, and middle-income groups alike.

Those concerned about the education of the "gifted" should be aware that switching funds to their education will create shortages elsewhere, and they should be at least prepared to make up the difference with tax increases.

Curriculum

Reading

If it were possible to make only one adjustment in the curriculum offered lower-income children, that adjustment might be made to greatest advantage in the reading program. Reading is *the* basic learning skill. It is the skill from which almost all academic learning flows. It is the skill that puts citizens in touch with the factual basis for making informed decisions. What is even more relevant, it is an almost indispensable requirement for upward movement through the social classes. It opens the door to better, higher-paying, pleasanter jobs and provides greater status and security with rising literacy levels.

As we have seen, lower-income students are particularly troubled by reading deficiencies. Unless the reading levels of these students are improved considerably—and the learning and language skills that derive from them—they will have little chance of competing with more literate students for desirable jobs.

No doubt an improper emphasis is often given to reading and to "book learning" in the schools. Reading is not the source of *all* knowledge. Without experience in the real world, book learning is often worth less than nothing; yet book learning, in large quantities, is an indispensable supplement to the knowledge of the real world. Many educators feel, quite properly, that "bookishness" is too exclusively prized in higher academic circles. This scale of values, they say with much accuracy, frequently produces "drones" who are good at chewing and regurgitating juiceless facts, but who have little imagination, individuality, independence, or real wisdom. All too often, they observe, schools have produced "prize" students with encyclopedic knowledge but without the character or creativity to survive in the world or to produce anything of real value.

What is worse, this lopsided and feverish pursuit of book learning and "intellectuality," to the exclusion of most other skills and virtues, often results in lopsided, warped, and anxiety-ridden personalities, as testified to by the high rates of suicide and mental illness found in very "intellectual" colleges. And sometimes it produces men such as Leopold and Loeb, whose ceiling-high scores on IQ and achievement tests hardly compensated for their moral and psychological deformities.

It is no doubt in reaction to this overemphasis on bookishness at the expense of other intellectual and moral qualities that many educators have tended to devaluate the reading skills and the central place of book learning in the curriculum. But, while this de-emphasis is perhaps desirable in some middle- and upper-income areas and with more advanced students, it does not seem at all proper in lower-income areas. It is an *absence* of bookishness rather than an *excess* of it that troubles lower-income students. It is not that they read too much; it is that they often don't read at all. This being true, there is little present danger that they will become too bookish; some few might, but the great majority are a long way from being saturated with book learning. Without highly developed reading skills and some close familiarity with the contents of books and other reading matter, there is small chance that lower-income children will ever be able to compete with upper-income children for the rewards of school and life.

Reading is often very poorly taught in the schools. English classes, perhaps more than others, are often dull, routine, and uninspiring, especially to boys who crave more action than they usually find in verbs. Yet, as many discover the hard way, reading can be a very stimulating experience when the reading situation is right and the reading material interesting and appropriate. In general, since all students have different tastes, it would seem that, once they have acquired elementary reading skills, they should be allowed to read what they want to read, with direction and encouragement from the teacher and a continuing exchange of information about books with other students.

Since boys seem especially bored with the fiction and the make-believe world of the average school storybook, they should be encouraged, as they seldom are, to follow their natural interest in sports pages and books, adventure stories, science fiction, simple biographies of vigorous males, and (in higher grades) books that deal frankly with the facts of life. Once they have developed the reading habit, they might even be willing to explore the teachers' nice Victorian world of *Silas Marner, David Copperfield, Ivanhoe, Jane Eyre, Little Women,* etc.— though this may be too much to expect. It is *not* too much to expect, however, that reading be made as attractive as possible for students, a task that will involve violating some of the Mid-Victorian taboos, giving students much freedom of choice, encouraging them to read pocket-size books (which they much prefer to hard-cover editions), and making all reading and learning facilities as pleasant as possible. Recordings and films from books should be used to stimulate interest in these books, since book sales indicate that nothing sells a book like a movie-version.

The library should be a focal point of the school, attractive, easy to use, accessible to students at all times, and continuing instruction should be given in library use for research and general reading purposes.

As part of the English program, continuing instruction should also be given in reading, study, and homework skills, with more direct attention to an unexplainably neglected skill—concentration, a prerequisite for all productive mental activity and one that bothers lower-status students more than others, as study has shown.

Much more attention should be directed to the critical period when students first learn to read, and to the phonics versus word-recognition controversy. Needless to say, battle positions should not be assumed until all evidence is in, and an offensive or defensive posture in relation to criticisms of the school reading program should not be an automatic one. To aid in beginning reading, perhaps students can be assigned from higher grades to tutor beginning students, particularly those who are not helped at home.

Many educators feel that broadening the life experiences of underprivileged students through trips and other excursions into the real world will make them more familiar with the vocabulary and subject matter of books and thereby improve their reading skills. Lloyd and Warfel are of this opinion: "The way to build your vocabulary is to build your experience, moving much among men and women and taking interest in their interests. . . ." [1]

Most texts used by lower-income students are totally alien to their vocabulary, experience, and interest. More suitable texts must be found, and where they cannot be found they must be *created*. Often texts are so bad that teachers in training must be given special instructions in how to *avoid* using them.

Bold experiments should be tried.

At Yale University, Omar Khayyam Moore, a sociologist, has been teaching two-year-olds to read, write, and type.[2] Within six months he gets them reading at second-grade level. His methods are totally permissive, rather than compulsory and painful. He simply lets the child "play" with an electric typewriter. The child strikes keys, and the instructor names the character printed. The instructor also projects the chosen letters on a screen. The child types for a half-hour and then prints the letters on a black-board. Soon he works up to complete words and eventually to sentences.

The child's learning is indirectly "controlled." His fingernails are painted various colors, and so are the keys corresponding to the fingers that should hit them. "What lures the child on is the sense of discovering the rules him-self." When they do so "their interest and excitement are almost without bounds." Equipment is now being designed to simplify the technique. The desirability of teaching children to read at age two may be questionable, but the techniques are interesting and imaginative.

To many lower-income children public libraries are grim, forbidding places, "conspiracies against the poor," in Sean O'Casey's words.

In Big City, libraries in upper-income areas stay open weekends. In lower-income areas, many of them close. The explanation given: children in these areas do not use the libraries. If they do not use the libraries, they must be actively encouraged to do so, and the libraries must remain open in order to permit them to do so. Above all, the library must be a place where they feel welcome and com-fortable and where they can find interesting and attractive books to read.

Whatever approaches are used, whatever methods are tried, certainly a situation should not be tolerated in which large numbers of lower-income children spend eight to ten years in school without having acquired high levels of reading and derivative language skills.

Aside from those who have suffered brain damage and those so deeply disturbed as to be beyond reach, no child should be permitted to leave school without having achieved normal facility in reading. The child who does not learn to read in school has been cheated and is almost inevitably doomed to social exclusion and economic denial.

Teaching children to read at age two may be of very questionable value. Teaching them to read even at age six, as many suggest, *may* be premature. But they must be taught at some point, and they should be taught with as little compulsion and as much pleasure as possible.

Judge John T. McWilliams of the Michigan courts claims that prison records show reading retardation to be the "greatest single characteristic common to all inmates," regardless of economic status. Jackson prison records show, he says, that "although most inmates under twenty-five were in the 80 to 89 IQ bracket when admitted, their IQ went up as high as 110 after they were there," improved reading skill being the explanation. Then, perhaps too hopefully, he says: "Wouldn't it be strange and wonderful if the way to prevent drop-outs and delinquency was to teach them to read?"

It would be, but this is too much to expect; reading is not a cure-all; it *is* a cure, however, for at least some of our major educational ailments, and its healing potential should not be neglected.

Language

Teaching students to speak and write "proper" English can be an obstacle course of traps and barriers, some of them almost too big for the average teacher to hurdle.

The teacher can tell the student what "educated English" *is,* but even if she tells him well, she can't always make him want to *speak* it or *write* it. Though the teacher and the school may approve of "good" English, the student may not, depending on the experiences he has had with people who use it. Often he can be downright hostile to it, for reasons which Lloyd and Warfel have pointed out:

> The sound of educated English stirs in them (the underprivileged) something less than admiration. It is the language of the big shot, the shyster lawyer who gets them off but strips them of their possessions, the judge who browbeats them, the teacher who flunks them out of school, the doctor who parks his fishtailed Cadillac in the driveway, the social worker who pries into their personal affairs, the shavetail MP who locks them up for wearing battle dress in the rest area, the general who whizzes by in a jeep, throwing mud in all directions, the snotty salesgirl in the department store, the credit manager, the employment man—educated English is the language of all who push them around, take their money, dole out charity, and try to make them feel like 2 cents while they are doing it, with looks and comments on their clothes, their manners, their housekeeping, and their talk. Educated English is the contemptuous, audible, universal sneer of the haves for the have-nots.[3]

Yet the "have-nots" are sometimes willing to learn the sound of educated English. But teachers are not always prepared to teach it. None of the present methods in use seems effective at all in changing language, especially oral speech, habits. Perhaps new devices (such as tape recorders that will play back the student's voice) will be more persuasive and helpful.

Grammar

The subject occupying more time than any other in the typical English class is grammar. No one will deny that grammar has its place in the English class, and that it is especially to be welcomed at higher grade levels where students seek the kind of language enrichment offered by such exercises as sentence diagramming. But what is taught at the lower levels, to those students who are barely literate, is often totally out of place. And it takes up so much time that students have little left over for what counts—reading, writing, and oral speech. It is out of place because it usually has not a thing in the world to do with the language habits of students who study it or with the kind of errors they make. Moreover, when it is simply an exercise in language structure (as it is in most cases) it has few competitors in dullness, judging by the depths of student apathy to it. Even when grammar is related to language use, the relationship is seldom pointed out in texts or in class so that the student can see the sense in what he is learning. Usually there isn't much sense. Thus students are required to know about participial phrases, transitive and intransitive verbs, indirect objects, infinitives, substantive nouns, and many greater and lesser grammatical forms, when they are often not up to pronouncing the words, let alone using whatever knowledge is offered to improve their language.

The same thing is true of most instruction in language "usage." But, while grammar exercises seem designed to help no one, usage exercises seem designed to help only those students (usually from middle- and upper-income groups) who commit minor infractions of the rules. So it is that continuing references are made in texts to misplaced commas, the forms of "lie" and "lay," the use of "who" and "whom," dangling participles, etc., with a sprinkling of the grosser errors committed by lower-income students. Neither the texts nor the teachers seem prepared to deal seriously with deep-seated language problems. Very often teachers of lower-income students are not even aware of what these problems are, not having the time or the training to analyze language difficulties that are not dealt with in the text. Typically, English teachers will rely solely on the text (which of course is the same for all students), going through it systematically, but without any reference to what students need to know. And so it is that students are often given advanced training in language structure and usage when they cannot express a simple intelligible thought in writing.

As a beginning, some effort should be made to discover the exact nature of the language problem in various student groups—Negro, Southern white, Polish, Italian, "working-class" white, etc.—so that instruction could be tailor-made to their group and individual needs. Perhaps this would mean abandoning the grammar text completely in favor of special short-form exercises adapted to student problems.

Writing

Writing appears to be a woefully neglected activity in most English classes. With all the textbook exercises, there is seldom much time for writing. More than this, English teachers simply cannot handle the heavy burden of writing assignments. If a high-school teacher has 150 students (a typical class load), and these students write one theme a week, she will spend 37½ hours per week reviewing these papers—at the modest rate of 15 minutes per paper. And this 37½ hours of homework will be in addition to all the other out-of-school assignments she has. Yet students must write at least once a week to achieve even minimum competence.

Another complicating problem is that English teachers often have a sadly limited understanding of what "good" writing looks like, their view being that it's good if it does not begin with "and" or end with a preposition. Other than knowing these two rules (which are violated a thousand times a day by professional writers), they can usually spot spelling errors and run-on sentences, but much beyond this they are lost. What results in student themes, at best, is properly spelled, grammatical, but constipated and juiceless prose. This is particularly true of themes written by lower-income students, who finally master the rules but never learn how to write easily and expressively.

Other Problems

While reading improvement is of primary importance for lower-income students (and the other language problems that flow mainly out of reading deficiencies), there are many other matters to be dealt with and other curriculum adjustments to be made. Those that occur to us are given here. The list is not complete. Nor do we pretend that it is a blueprint. It is simply what seems reasonable to us under present circumstances.

Some of the suggestions are directly related to the problems of lower-income children. Some are more distantly related and are of more general application.

1. People who understand and sympathize with the problems of lower-income students should be elected to school boards. These people of course should also be imaginative and courageous enough to work out ways of handling such problems, or to hire people who can.

2. School administrators should not be selected, as they often seem to be at present, according to how innocuous and easy-going they are, but rather on the basis of energy, ambition, organizational skills, and ability to enlist the creative resources of teachers, students, and citizens. In other words, administrators should be more executive than professorial in temperament. Since there are a great many more women than men teachers to select administrators from, high-level administrative jobs should not be so exclusively limited to men as they now are.

3. Teachers with some zeal for teaching lower-income students should be encouraged to come into the profession.

4. Experimentation with television, teaching machines, and other educational devices should be encouraged in an effort to free teachers for individual and small-group work with students. Properly used, such devices can lift much of the burden of classroom overloading, lesson-planning, and discipline from teachers, while permitting them to do more creative and rewarding work with students.

5. Use of IQ tests should be stopped.

6. More attention should be given to the psychological, medical, and nutritional needs of lower-income students; where community agencies do not provide necessary services, the schools should feel obliged to take on the responsibility.

7. There should be warm encouragement of lower-income parents to meet with teachers on child-guidance matters and participate in school-parent activities.

8. The dead weight of meaningless dates and data should be removed from the curriculum and replaced with learning activities and knowledge that will be purposeful, meaningful, and intellectually stimulating. Education should begin with an inquiry into needs. What does the child *need* to know? What does society *need* to teach him —now and in the future? Not, what have we been teaching him for the past half-century? Not, what is in the textbook used in the course? Not what is in *any* text, or *any* book, necessarily? Not even, what will colleges require him to know?—for they too can be giant storage bins for dead knowledge.

Only—what does the child *need* to know, intellectually, socially, vocationally, morally? And, what are the urgent needs of society, to which the individual must make some contribution?

9. Class size in lower-income schools should be reduced.

10. Important instructional facilities should be equalized; where equalization is not made, compensation of other kinds should be given.

11. The distribution of qualified teachers should be equalized, or inequalities compensated for. In schools where it is difficult to get teachers, pay scales should be raised or other rewards provided.

12. All segregated groupings and curriculums, except those of a very temporary nature, should be eliminated.

13. Extra help, rather than failing marks, should be given those who fall behind.

14. The present highly competitive system of marks,

exams, and comparisons of all sorts should be replaced by other types of incentives to learn. If there is to be competition, emphasis should be on group rather than on individual competition. Marks and grades hurt more than they help; they discourage students from studying "hard" subjects or taking good but tough teachers; they discourage really independent and critical thinking, since the teacher who marks you cannot be questioned or challenged too much; and they tend to make "good" students conformists and "bad" students rebellious.

15. Though marks should be eliminated, the schools should be much more aware than they are now of the relative achievement levels of all students at all times. Students and parents—if they *want* to know—should be given exact information (in person rather than by report card) about how student achievement levels compare with others in the same school, in the same city, with national norms, and with the highest achieving areas of the community or the country. Nationally standardized achievement tests will provide a better basis for knowing where a student stands than the present marking system. Achievement-score averages of all *schools* (but not of individual students, of course) should be open to public inspection at all times, providing a continuous check on school progress.

16. The platoon system should be eliminated, in lower elementary-school grades especially. In Big City almost all elementary-school students now change home-room teachers every semester. Some school systems are experimenting with the ungraded primary school, in which students stay with the same teacher from beginning kindergarten through the first three grades. Such a system, it is claimed, gives the child more security and provides an opportunity

for the teacher, during these critical years, to get to know all about her students and their problems and needs.

17. Special attention should be given to the homework problem in lower-income high schools. Where home conditions are not conducive to study, homework presents a very troublesome problem for students. The citizens' committee in Big City has recommended that homework be increased; if this is indeed advisable, then lower-income students should be given special instruction in study and homework skills, and time should be allowed for students to do homework assignments in school—in study hall, or during a lengthened class period.

18. It should not be assumed that lower-income students cannot (or should not, for one reason or another) master a foreign language or other courses required for college entrance. With modern methods of teaching language, it might turn out that lower-income students would enjoy the study of a foreign language and that such study might help them master English.

19. The lower-income students' range of experience with the outside world should be broadened by means of field trips.

20. Perhaps efforts should be made to work out a system in which students proceed through school as fast as they reasonably can. At the same time, special attention should be given to those who move slowly. It must be kept in mind always, of course, that the individual child is what counts in school. In most American schools, certainly in Big City schools, the individual child and his personal needs are grossly neglected. The school and the teacher are simply too busy to spend any time with him. If the rights of the individual are to be observed at all in our

schools, then some means must be devised for freeing teachers or providing other personnel for individual consultation with students.

21. More opportunity should be provided for students to work on individual and group projects.

22. Wherever it seems advisable, students should be given a voice in planning their own goals and programs of study. It is an educational truism that students learn more, with greater eagerness and less need for control and discipline, when they pursue their own goals rather than others' and when they have some voice in determining what they will do and what they will learn. Obviously it is easy to go too far in this direction, since students are often incapable of making decisions about what they should do, or even what they *want* to do; but where they are able and willing they should be given this valuable experience in independent decision-making.

Moving away from dull, pointless routines dictated by the teacher, into work on projects of their own choice, solving real problems in real-life situations, will make learning more stimulating and more rewarding for lower-income students. Learning of this kind, then, will be directed toward problem-solving rather than the simple memorization of facts. Under present conditions of classroom overcrowding, of course, such an approach to education is usually difficult, often impossible.

23. Free textbooks should be provided, all other student costs reduced or eliminated.

24. There should be more work-study programs. At the same time, purely vocational training should be de-emphasized in the schools, since this training often becomes obsolete before it can be used. Also, special "trade" and

"vocational" schools should be discontinued, unless the vocational curriculum is liberal in approach and broad in character. Such schools are often used as dumping grounds for students who are not wanted elsewhere, and often little more than custodial care is provided in them. Where more is provided, the skills taught are frequently of too perishable a nature.

25. Ways of stimulating "school spirit" in lower-income students should be worked out.

26. As for extra-curricular activities, there should be more emphasis on sports, and recreational and cultural activities that will involve *all* students rather than a select few. The sports program, especially, should not be so exclusive as it is now; all boys who want to play should be put on teams.

27. Since classroom discipline seems to produce more headaches for teachers than anything else, new approaches to the discipline problem must be made. Methods now used—scoldings, low marks, failures, and sometimes, very unfortunately, even corporal punishment—apparently do not work with a great many students, and in fact seem to have an effect opposite to what is presumably intended.

Group projects and group planning are excellent learning devices. Yet they are hard to use in the typical classroom because of the commotion and discipline problems that can result. Adjustments should be made in room equipment, room size, and class size to make such projects easier to handle. Groups, working with a purpose, can often discipline themselves without teacher interference.

28. Techniques for teaching *self*-discipline to students, in a direct rather than an indirect way, should be devised. Students should learn the value of self-discipline (the

body, mind, and impulses), and some of the techniques for achieving self-mastery and self-control. This area has not been explored much by educators, or by anyone else for that matter, except in so far as self-discipline is applied indirectly by forces outside the individual.

29. There should be a special staff to provide a *full range* of occupational information to lower-income students, such information sessions beginning well before high school.

30. The educational and occupational aspirations of lower-income students should be raised by convincing them that they can and should continue in school—even into college. Students should be convinced that education can be extremely useful and valuable to them in later life, and that advanced levels of education are usually necessary to qualify for many of the rewards of adult life (higher income, easier and more rewarding work, greater prestige, more security, broader participation in social, cultural, and intellectual life, etc.).

31. There should be special group and individual counseling sessions to convince lower-income students they should not drop out of school.

32. Curriculum materials ought not to be so fixed that teachers cannot change them or reject them, but a great deal more assistance should be given teachers in lesson-planning and in organizing a classroom. Certainly at the high-school level no single teacher has the time or the talent to work out really stimulating programs for five or six different classes of students every day. As a result many classes are routine, dreary, and quite unproductive.

Teachers can learn from the long experiences of other teachers by means of rather specific lesson-plan guides

which they can use, or modify for use, as they see fit. Many
educators object to the use of standardized materials, however, claiming that they are the principal source of
monotony and neglect of individual needs in the classroom. But perhaps it is more the *mis*use, rather than the
use, of standardized materials that produces these undesirable results. When materials are first-rate and when they
are used flexibly, they can provide a much more stimulating classroom situation than would otherwise be possible.
They can also provide the teacher with more time and
more freedom to attend to the individual needs of students.

33. Less time should be spent arguing about education
at the theoretical and philosophical level, and more time
perfecting techniques for achieving goals which are uni-
versally agreed upon. Perhaps if all sides can give John
Dewey a brief rest as an authority on what should or
should not be done in the schools, time can then be spent
using his pragmatic scientific approach to solve some of
our obvious and agreed-upon school problems.

34. The work load of teachers must be reduced. As it
is, the average high-school teacher, for example, may teach
five, even six, different classes a day. In addition, he must
do his own clerical work, keep attendance, devise frequent
tests, read in his field, correct papers, counsel with students, attend meetings, serve on committees, spend a period on hall or lunchroom duty—and make out five separate exciting and challenging lessons plans. Obviously,
under these conditions, whatever excitement there is in
class is purely accidental.

The college professor, on the other hand, thinks he is
overworked (and usually *is*) if he teaches *ten* hours of class

a week. The high-school teacher has twenty-five to thirty hours of class a week.

35. Efforts should be made to encourage more men, of a type boys can readily identify with, to enter teaching. Such efforts are being made to some extent in Big City schools and elsewhere. Problem schools in low-income areas of Big City now often have a majority of male teachers in them.

36. Children in problem areas should be reached by the schools as quickly as possible. Nursery-school care should be provided as preparation for school and as relief for the working mother.

37. The general "feeling tone" of the schools should be one of love, encouragement, stimulation, equality, rather than high-pressure competition, snobbery, authoritarianism, and cold, impersonal external discipline. Yet it must not be passive, but very active, alert, and aggressive. It should be soft-hearted, in short, but very hard-headed.

Further Research

Much is suspected but little is known about numbers of factors bearing upon social class distinctions in the school, factors which are more intangible than school buildings, facilities, services, etc., in that they depend on the mental attitudes and viewpoints of those associated with the schools, and indeed often on the goals and general nature of the entire society.

Except for sources cited in this study there appears to be a serious shortage of information about teacher, parent, administrator, and student attitudes as they relate to social class.

We do not know enough (or in some cases *anything*) about the attitudes of different income and ethnic groups toward their children, the schools, or educational matters in general; nor do we know what they value and what they regard as important and worth doing.

We do not know enough about child-rearing practices: Do some groups train their children to be aggressive and to take leadership, while others restrain their children and train them to be followers? What methods of control and restraint are used; is control exercised through love or through punishment? Are some families more mother-dominated and more female in outlook than others? How much is "masculinity" valued by various groups, and what is regarded as masculine behavior? What differences are there in the sexual codes and sexual interests of various groups, and what influence do these have on their life-goals and school behavior? What role does sexual aggressiveness play in the high drop-out rate of lower-income boys and their delinquent behavior?

Does the puritanism of the school repel lower-income boys and cause them to go elsewhere for information that interests them? It is possible for active, athletic boys to apply themselves to learning, to be as scholarly, as boys who are less active physically; in other words, how compatible are physical and mental activity?

How do various family groups train their children to react to authority? Does home training encourage children to respect authority, accept it, fear it, confront it, butter-up to it, or rebel against it?

What manners and social graces are taught and practiced in various groups; what, specifically, are the manners and style of dress, speech, and behavior of upper-status groups, and how unacceptable are other styles of living to them?

Why is it that children at some economic levels who come from broken homes appear to do better in school than those from homes in which the father is present?

How much does the school value obedience and the quieter, more conformist virtues?

The Female School

Related to a great many of these questions is the matter of what we may call "the female school," the school that is run largely by and for the female of the human species. Though it was reported recently that for the first time in modern history there are more men than women in public junior and senior high schools, women still dominate overwhelmingly the public elementary schools attended by the great bulk of school-age children.

Taken on an average, girls do much better in school than boys—either because they mature faster physically or because the schools make it easier for them to succeed, or both. By almost any measurement used, they do much better; they get better grades, more honors and awards, and much better citizenship ratings.

In Big City three times as many boys as girls are failed. Since failures are found mostly in lower-income groups, this means that lower-income boys are having a worse time of it in school than any other category of students.

Also, in Big City a great many more boys than girls are sent to the city's Detention Home (and later to prison); similarly, delinquency rates are much higher among boys than among girls. It appears that this superiority of girls in school does not always exist in upper-income schools, where boys tend to be highly motivated to do well in school; also, at the college level, boys (mostly from upper-income families at this level) tend to have a margin over girls, probably because girls are not driven by the same occupational necessities.

It has been observed that school culture is typically "polite, prissy, and puritanical" and that there is little place in this female culture for some of the high-ranking values of boy-culture—courage, loyalty, independence—or the high-ranking interests of boys—sports (except in gym class), outdoor life, popular music, adventure, sex, action.

Teachers, whose gender is usually feminine, seem to favor girls over boys; they understand their needs and interests better and they tend to be much more approving of their quiet, polite, docile behavior. For women teachers, girls are usually much easier to handle, the boys being often regarded as roughnecks who talk back and won't do as they're told.

Boys, in their turn, are likely to think of "good behavior," viewed by female school standards, as being sissy —and nothing is to be avoided with greater caution by many of these boys than sissy behavior. And so it is that many boys, especially as they begin their pre-adolescent struggle for independence and manhood, reject the good behavior of the school and its "prissy" standards of conduct, just as the school has rejected them for their roughneck behavior. Thus the struggle between boy and school grows with the passing school years.

Unfortunately the question of the female school has never been very deeply probed, very likely because it is too sensitive a subject for examination. Yet for lower-income boys, who have more trouble in school than other groups and who tend to be more concerned about "manliness" than about any other virtues, it is a very significant educational problem and one that deserves much fuller exploration. Perhaps vitalizing the curriculum and hiring more male teachers of a type that can command the respect and admiration of boys will help make school and lower-income male culture more compatible.

The Eager Ones

More research is needed on the reaction of some lower-income groups to the obvious "apple polisher," the "eager beaver," the "teacher's pet"—to the children who eagerly seek the teacher's approval, do much more than is required, tattle on classmates, obey all orders and requests, and who are generally very successful in school.

Indications are that—because of the heavy emphasis in the schools on competition and teacher-approval—these "eager beavers" are often held in contempt by their peers. If there were less emphasis on these things and less approval given to apple-polishing, perhaps the eager ones would be much more acceptable to their classmates, and perhaps those who now reject this often senseless scrambling for favor and honors would become more eager about their own school work.

This competitive scramble is often a senseless and self-defeating one because it does not call forth the best in students—either morally or scholastically. Very often the scramble involves doing "more" rather than doing "better," and buttering-up the teacher rather than challenging her on basic issues when questions of truth and justice (especially classroom justice) are concerned.

Research has shown that the main factor in awarding

high marks and honors in school is "extra work"—not superior work, but extra work. Cramer found in a study of teachers' perceptions of brightness roles that extra work by students was the most commonly recognized criterion of superiority.[4]

This extra work is often little more than pointless busy work, involving endless hours of unproductive labor and resulting in a highly competitive mass-production system that often verges on the ridiculous.

As witness to the purposelessness of many extra work projects, the author is reminded of her own high school World History class, in which A and B grades were awarded according to the number of maps handed in! The maps were all copied, of course, or traced, or filled in on a printed form as one colors a child's picture book, but the fact that nothing creative went into the job and no learning came out of it did not deter either the teacher or the students. Not a single word of protest was raised by these "eager" students about this busy work. In fact there was such a scurry of map-making activity that by the end of the semester the teacher had been deluged with thousands of maps, the winner producing over two hundred—all undoubtedly going, unexamined, into the wastebasket, along with most other school busy work.

If any achievement standard is to be set up in the schools, it might more properly be based on how much a child has learned, and how much he has created, rather than how much work he has done and how many hours he spent doing it.

Of course everyone would agree that one of the major jobs of the schools is to encourage students to pursue learning eagerly and independently and without continual pressure from the teacher. But present methods are apparently producing the opposite effect in lower-income children, since these children seem to become less interested and more hostile to the "eager beaver" mentality the longer they are exposed to it.

An incentive system that would be a real intellectual challenge to students—rather than an empty, purely competitive one—might produce the desired eagerness for learning in lower-income children.

Rewards

Further research is also needed on the rewards and punishments to which lower-income children will respond. Evidence is, as we have mentioned, that rewards offered in the present incentive system do not excite much response in many lower-income children, the principal rewards being report-card marks and teacher-parent approval. Frequently students do not respond to these rewards because they realize there is little chance of getting them. Often they do not respond because they do not know what the rewards are worth—either now or in later life. They do not respond because they are often so at odds with both teachers and parents that they are more likely to seek their disapproval than their approval.

In order to provide suitable rewards, it would be of great value to the schools to have systematic information about the needs and natural interests of lower-income children, by ethnic and racial sub-groups.

College Studies

Studies parallel to this one should be made of inequalities in college and university education. Since curriculum standards in public schools are often laid down by college requirements (initiated at the graduate-school level often: see Earl McGrath, *The Graduate School and the Decline of Liberal Education*), and since college admission practices and opportunities for college success have a profound effect on what happens to students in public schools, the subject would seem to require a large-scale investigation.

Open Records

The records of individual schools, upon which this study is based, are not open to general public review, and in fact were made available for this study only with considerable reluctance.

These records are closed to public inspection, it is said, because information that would permit a comparison of schools might cause embarrassment to the students in these schools, and might also cause considerable difficulty in the community.

It is easy to see that such things might happen if records were made public; it is *not* easy to see, however, that these consequences would be damaging to the schools in the long run. Some immediate embarrassment might be caused for students in low-ranking schools, but the knowledge that they are low-ranking might help to improve their standing. Also, such knowledge would undoubtedly result in pressure on administrators to improve conditions and performance levels in some schools. Making these records public, and arousing public concern about conditions in specific schools, might be the only way to improve conditions in low-ranking schools.

Parents and citizens have a right to know how their school compares with other schools in the same school district, or with schools elsewhere in the country. They have as much right to know this as they have to know how their children compare with other children in the same class or school, facts which the school does not hesitate to tell them. It is strange, and perhaps revealing, that the schools put so much emphasis on comparisons and competition between individual *students,* and yet are so opposed to any kind of comparisons between individual *schools.* Comparisons between schools would appear to be much less damaging to students than comparisons between individuals, and it is very possible that such school comparisons might do much more than individual comparisons to raise performance levels of these students—and also performance levels of school administrators and school personnel.

If these records cannot be suddenly opened to the public, then perhaps as a first step they can be opened for review by a selected group of interested citizens.

Experimental Programs

There perhaps would be some differences of opinion about what specific goals a program of education for underprivileged children should pursue. It would seem likely, however, that there would be general agreement about these two broad objectives: education for lower-income children that would provide such skills and understandings as would enable them to compete as far as possible on the same levels with upper-income children for the rewards of school and of later life; education that would equip them to function as useful citizens in a democracy and to lead richer fuller lives.

If experimental programs aimed at these objectives are to achieve maximum success, it will require that they be bold and imaginative and that they incorporate all reasonable ideas from the widest possible variety of sources and points of view. The invitation to new ideas (from whatever source) would mean that all presently fixed ideas about what education should be might better be converted into tentative ideas, to be tested alongside a great variety of conflicting ideas. It is very possible that the most effective program of education for underprivileged children has not yet been tried out or even suggested, and so it would seem advisable in an experimental program to welcome all ideas, old or new, from sources inside and outside the schools, and to exhaust all possibilities in an effort to provide the best possible education for lower-income children, and indeed for all children.

The evidence seems to indicate that such experimental programs should provide a style of education that is packed with present and future meaning for the average student.

It should be a style that appeals to the very practical, though inquiring and searching, mind of the typical American student, a style that meets him where he is, with his heritage of tastes and interests, and leads him to a richer range of interests.

Certainly it should not be a style of education that says: "We have all the answers; we have the perfectly refined tastes; we will tell you what to do, what to like, and you must either accept it or give up your dream of being 'educated.' "

Students know much more than we think they know—
even those from the lowest status levels in our society.
Their tastes, their interests are often more alive and more
vibrant than their teachers' and more in keeping with the
times. The older generation cannot impose its exact image
on the younger generations, any more than "elite" groups
can impose their ways on the "masses." Nor would such an
imposition necessarily be desirable, even if it were possible.
History shows that many of the great innovations in culture and the arts had their origin in mass tastes, so the
elite cannot be too smug about its record.

Certainly there should be more exchange, more give and
take between the teacher and the learner. We must listen
to the younger generations and make a serious effort to
understand what they are saying. We should find out what
their needs are and what they would like to learn. If they
want to learn about jet planes, we should not insist upon
Latin grammar.

Unlike the "gifted" child, who will more often do
what he is told to do, learn what he is told to learn, the
"average" child demands education that is challenging
and packed with meaning, and he will not participate in
the educational process unless he gets it.

Progress in education seems to move very slowly. Perhaps this can be attributed to the fact that educators are
often uncertain about what to do or how to do it. But, in
addition, there seems to be a strong tendency among many
educators to resist changes in the old ways of doing things,
while clinging uncertainly to the educational status quo.
Like most people, they tend to feel more comfortable
with things as they are, fearing that changes might impose
additional burdens on them or threaten their job security.

Of course some of these fears are justified by the actual results of some experimental programs. But very often these fears, especially when they arise before programs are even tried out, are more in the nature of reflex actions than reasonable apprehensions. When such irrational fears have been in control of large blocks of opinion, they have often seriously impeded educational progress, obstructing all but the most minor changes in school organization. As a result, the reputation of educators has been injured, and the educational enrichment and stimulation such programs could provide have been denied to both teachers and students.

Some of this opposition to innovation is directed against changes in "what a teacher does in the classroom," some of it against basic revisions in school organization, and some of it against the introduction of new tools and techniques of teaching. In fact it seems that—from one source or another—there is rather serious opposition to almost all suggested changes in what the schools are doing. And every educational point of view seems to have some area of irrational opposition to innovation.

If education is to take new and better directions, then some way must be found of either allaying such irrational fears or pushing on in spite of them. It should also be added that, if these new directions are to be pursued, school leaders and administrators will need to call upon all available sources of courage and imagination within themselves and within others. Perhaps an insufficiency of these qualities has been as responsible as anything else for the lag in educational progress.

Our schools have been under rather heavy assault in recent years, often from the wrong directions and for the wrong reasons. The attacks have been led in many cases by elite guards who want to constrict education and put "Authority" back in the classroom.

Many educators have reacted defensively to these criticisms, as is quite proper. The reaction, however, has become almost a reflex, the defensiveness almost indiscriminate.

Our schools are the nation's most vital resource. What happens there will affect the fate of the nation and the fate of every individual child. To make the American dream a reality, to realize the full potential of our nation and *all* its citizens, we must enlist the full support of our schools, we must recognize that they are not doing the job they should be doing, and we must welcome all constructive criticisms and suggestions for reform.

Democracy and education for *all* are inseparably linked. As Thomas Mann has observed: "Democracy wishes to elevate mankind, to teach it to think, to set it free. It seeks to remove from culture the stamp of privilege and disseminate it among the people—in a word, it aims at education."

NOTES

CHAPTER 1

1. Ward, Lester, *Applied Sociology*. Boston and New York: Ginn, 1906.

CHAPTER 2

1. Toby, Jackson, "Orientation to Education as a Factor in the School Maladjustment of Lower-Class Children." *Social Forces,* vol. 35, no. 3, March 1957.
2. Kahl, Joseph A., "Educational and Occupational Aspirations of Common-Man Boys." *The Harvard Educational Review,* vol. 23, no. 3, Summer 1953.
3. Becker, Howard S. "Social Class Variations in the Teacher-Pupil Relationship." *Journal of Educational Sociology,* vol. 25, no. 8, April 1952.
4. Strang, Ruth M., "Reading Development of Gifted Children." *Elementary English,* 31, January 1954.
5. Gray, William S., "Summary of Reading Investigations." *Journal of Educational Research,* 51, February 1958.
6. Coleman, H. A., "The Relationship of Socio-Economic Status to the Performance of Junior High School Students." *Journal of Experimental Education,* 9, September 1940.
7. Milner, Esther, "A Study of the Relationship between Reading Readiness in Grade 1 School Children and Patterns of Parent-Child Interaction." *Child Development,* 22, June 1951.

8. Bereday, George E., Teachers College, Columbia University, New York City, as reported in *The New York Times*, May 4, 1958.

9. Burton, William H., "Education and Social Class in the United States." *Harvard Educational Review*, vol. 23, no. 4, Fall 1953.

10. Hecker, S. E., *Early School Leavers in Kentucky*. Lexington: University of Kentucky, 1953. Seay, M. F., McGlothlin, W. J., *Elementary Education in Two Communities of the Tennessee Valley*. Bureau of School Service, University of Kentucky, vol. XIV, no. 3, March 1942. Meece, L. E., Adams, H. P., Eckel, H., Hooper, R. L., *Twenty-Five Years of Service to Kentucky's Schools*. Bureau of School Service, University of Kentucky, vol. XXV, no. 2, December 1952.

11. Handlin, Oscar, *The Uprooted*. New York: Grosset & Dunlap, 1957.

12. Davis, Allison, "Socio-Economic Influences upon Children's Learning." Speech delivered at the Midcentury White House Conference on Children and Youth, National Guard Armory, Washington, D.C., December 5, 1950.

13. Hollingshead, August B., *Elmtown's Youth*. New York: John Wiley, 1949.

14. Murcell, James T., *Psychological Testing*. New York: Longmans, 1947.

15. Lloyd, Donald J., and Warfel, Harry R., *American Language and Its Cultural Setting*. New York: Knopf, 1956.

16. Vernon, P. E., "Coaching for All Advised." *The* (London) *Times Education Supplement*, February 1, 1952, and December 12, 1952.

17. Newman, H. H., Freeman, F. N., Holzinger, K. J., *Twins: A Study of Heredity and Environment*. Chicago: University of Chicago, 1937.

18. "In a Space Age Community: Tomorrow's Schools Today." *U.S. News and World Report*, 47, October 12, 1959.

19. Davis, Allison, op. cit.

20. *New Republic*, September 12, 1960, p. 6.

21. Drews, E. N. Speech at Michigan State University, East Lansing, as reported in the *Ann Arbor News*, May 27, 1958.

22. Witty, Paul, *The Gifted Child*. American Association for Gifted Children. Boston: Heath, 1951.

23. Hersey, John, *The Child Buyer*. New York: Knopf, 1960.

24. Young, Michael D., *The Rise of the Meritocracy*. London: Thames & Hudson, 1958.

25. *Kiplinger's Magazine,* April 1958.
26. Bond, Horace Mann, "The Productivity of National Merit Scholars by Occupational Class." *School and Society,* 85, September 28, 1957.
27. Terman, Lewis M., et al., "Mental and Physical Traits of a Thousand Gifted Children." *Genetic Studies of Genius,* vol. I, Stanford: Stanford University, 1925. Hollingsworth, Leta S., *Gifted Children, Their Nature and Nurture.* New York: Macmillan, 1926. Terman, Lewis M., and Oden, Melita, "The Gifted Child Grows Up." *Genetic Studies of Genius,* vol. IV, Stanford: Stanford University, 1947. Ibid., "The Significance of Deviates, III: Correlates of Adult Achievement in the California Gifted Group." *Intelligence,* 39th Yearbook, Part I, NSSE, Public School, 1940. Adams, Fay, and Brown, Walker, *Teaching the Bright Pupil.* New York: Holt, 1930.
28. Carriker, William R., and Asher, William, "Research Related to Pupils with Special Abilities." *School Life,* February 1960.
29. Gallagher, James J., and Crowder, Thora H., "Adjustment of Gifted Children in the Regular Classroom." *Educating the Gifted,* Joseph L. French, New York: Holt, 1959.
30. Welles, Sam, "The Jewish Elan." *Fortune,* February 1960.
31. Slocomb, Herline, "The Myth of Neglect." *Clearing House,* 29, 1955.
32. Havighurst, Robert J., "Knowledge of Class Status Can Make a Difference." *Progressive Education,* vol. 27, no. 4, February 1950.
33. Johnson, Arthur C., "Our Schools Make Criminals." *Journal of Criminal Law and Criminology,* vol. 33, no. 4, 1942.
34. Cohen, Albert (Professor of Sociology at Indiana University), speech at Michigan State University.
35. Loeb, Martin B., "Implications of Status Differentiation for Personal and Social Development." *Harvard Educational Review,* vol. 23, no. 3, Summer 1953.
36. Burton, William H., "Educational and Social Class in the United States." *Harvard Educational Review,* vol. 23, no. 4, Fall 1953.
37. Davis, Allison, "The Motivation of the Underprivileged Worker." *Industry and Society,* New York: McGraw-Hill, 1947.
38. Abrahamson, S., "Our Status System and Scholastic Rewards." *Journal of Educational Sociology,* vol. 25, no. 8, April 1952.
39. Hollingshead, August B., op. cit.
40. Mitchell, James V., Jr., "Identification of Items in the California

Test of Personality that Differentiate Between Subjects of High and Low Socio-Economic Status at the Fifth and Seventh Grade Levels." *Journal of Educational Research,* 51, December 1957.
41. Krugman, Judith I., "Cultural Deprivation and Child Development." *High Points,* 38, November 1956.
42. Arnow, Harriette, *The Dollmaker.* New York: Macmillan, 1954.

CHAPTER 3

1. Krugman, Judith I., op. cit.
2. Volberding, E., "Out of School Living of 11 Year Old Boys and Girls from Differing Socio-Economic Groups." *Elementary School Journal,* vol. XLIX, no. 6, February 1949.

CHAPTER 4

1. Bond, Horace Mann, op. cit.
2. Hollingshead, August B., op. cit.
3. Abrahamson, S., op. cit.
4. Durham, R., and Cole, E. S., "Social Class Structure in Emporia Senior High School." *Midwest Sociologist,* vol. XIX, no. 2, May 1957.
5. Stouffer, Samuel A., "The Student—Problems Related to the Use of Academic Ability." *The Identification and Education of the Academically Talented Student in the American Secondary School,* The Conference Report, NEA, February 1958.
6. Hollingshead, August B., op. cit.
7. Warner, W. Lloyd, Havighurst, R. J., Loeb, N. B., *Who Shall Be Educated?* New York: Harper, 1944.
8. Smith, Margaret Ruth, "A Study of First Year Drop Outs" (entered September 1953).
9. Packard, Vance, *The Status Seekers.* New York: McKay, 1959.
10. *How People Pay for College.* Ann Arbor, Michigan: Survey Research Center, 1960.
11. *The New York Times,* April 5, 1959.
12. Moon, Rexford G., Jr., *The New York Times,* April 5, 1959.
13. Kahl, Joseph A., op. cit.
14. Stouffer, Samuel A., op. cit.
15. Warner, W. Lloyd, Havighurst, R. J., Loeb, N. B., op. cit.

16. McGrath, Earl G., *Improving School Holding Power*. Washington: US Office of Education, 1951, no. 291.

17. Dresher, Richard H., "Factors in Voluntary Drop-out in Public Secondary Schools of Detroit, Michigan." Unpublished dissertation, Oregon State College, 1953.

18. Lynd, Robert S. and Helen M., *Middletown, A Study in American Culture*. New York: Harcourt, Brace, 1929.

19. Hand, Harold C., *Principles of Public Secondary Education*. New York: Harcourt, Brace, 1958.

20. Montague, Joel B., "Social Status and Adjustment in School," *Clearing House*, 27, September 1952.

21. *Life,* May 9, 1960.

CHAPTER 5

1. Sims, V. M. "Social Class Affiliation of a Group of Public School Teachers," *School Review,* 59, September 1951. Study comparisons made with classifications of Centers, Richard, *The Psychology of Social Classes*. Princeton: Princeton University, 1949.

2. Handlin, Oscar, op. cit.

3. Caughran, Roy W., "School Board Members Today." *American School Board Journal,* 133, November–December 1956.

4. Havighurst, Robert J., op. cit.

5. Warner, W. Lloyd, and associates, *Democracy in Jonesville*. New York: Harper, 1949.

CHAPTER 6

1. Clark, Kenneth B., "Desegregation: The Role of the Social Sciences." *Teachers College Record,* vol. 62, no. 1, October 1960.

2. Lipset, Seymour Martin, "The British Voter—II; Sex, Age and Education." *The New Leader,* November 21, 1960.

CHAPTER 7

1. Lloyd and Warfel, op. cit.

2. *Time,* November 7, 1960.

3. Lloyd and Warfel, op. cit.

4. Cramer, Charles N. "An Inquiry into Teacher and Superior Pupil Perceptions of Brightness Roles," unpublished dissertation, University of Maryland, 1957.

INDEX

Ability groups, 198, 199; high-school, 152, 194–97
Abrahamson, S., on high school social system, 170; study of school rewards, 82–84
Achievement levels, 269
Adult education: costs, 254; elementary, 113; evening school enrollments, 167
Arithmetic achievement scores, 29
Arnow, Harriette, quotation from *The Dollmaker*, 109–11
Attendance: elementary school, 98–99; high school, 157
Attendance officers, 254

Becker, Howard, on skills gap of deprived children, 28
Bereday, George E., remedial reading experiment, 32–33
Berelson, Bernard, on graduate student backgrounds, 193–94
"Big City," identification of, 5
Bond, Horace Mann, Merit Scholar study, 64, 160–62
Bronx High School of Science, 66
Buildings and facilities: appearances, 130; elementary school, 122–34; high school, 215–22;

healthfulness, 129–30; rating tables, 131–34; safety, 129; 253
Burton, William H., on middle-class culture, 78; on textbooks, 35–36

California Test of Personality, 89–94
Cape Canaveral intelligence tests, 49–50
Caughran, Roy W., on school board representation, 235–36
Clark, Kenneth B., on segregation, 243–44
Class, social: and ability groups, 196, 197; and clubs, 169–71; and (high school) curricula, 176, 179, 180; definition of, 10–11; discrimination, 16–17; (high school) distinctions, 151–53; and income, 13; and reading, 31–32, 35; and scholarships, 161–62; structure, 18
Class size, elementary school, 113–115; high school, 212–13; 268
Clubs, 167–71, 254
Cohen, Albert, on delinquency, 76
Cole, C. S., on Emporia high school clubs, 170–71
Coleman, H. A., on reading and social class, 31

294

College: admissions, 187–88; drop-outs, 181; and intelligence tests, 190–91; preparation for, 81–82, 182–93, 273, 282

College Scholarship Service, 186, 187

Combs, Arthur W., on intelligence, 49–50

Continuous class programs, 213–14

Cooperative Research Program, U.S. Office of Education, 66

Cramer, on incentives, 280

Crowther report, 248

Curricula: elective, 173–74; high school, 152–53, 171–73, 174, 176, 177–80; materials, 273–74; segregation by, 272

Davis, Allison, on validity of intelligence tests, 40, 50; on middle-class culture, 79

Delinquency: elementary school, 69–81; high school, 164–65; and jobs, 158; and reading, 262; 141–144

Democracy in Jonesville, quotation, from, 236

Detention Home, 71

Detention School: costs of service, 255; high-school admissions, 164–165; 70, 71, 72, 73

Diphtheria, 100

Discipline, 85–86, 272, 273

Disturbed children, 87–95

Dollmaker, The, quotation from, 109–11

Dresher, Richard H., on drop-out causes, 203

Drews, E. N., on gifted children, 61

Drop-outs, college, 181, 185, 189–90

Drop-outs, elementary school, 97

Drop-outs, high school: causes, 204–208; costs, 253; by income groups, 202; Montague study, 206–208; savings from, 202; solutions to problem, 208–10; tables, 201; 153, 199–201

Durham, R., on Emporia high school clubs, 170–71

Edwards, T. B., study of gifted, 64

Elections, school-board, 236–37

Employment: and college preparation, 184; opportunities, 157–58

English language, failures, 163–64; teaching, 262–66

Environment and reading, 32

Environment, home, 139–47

"ESRPS," *see* Teachers, substitute

Ethnic groups: attitudes toward college, 193; and gifted, 66; school-board representation, 235, 236

Evening school costs, 254

Expenses, high school student, 204–206

Extracurricular activities, 83–84

Failures, high school, 162–64

Family influence, 85

Federal aid, 255–56

Field trips, 146–47, 260, 270

First Grade Intelligence test, Big City, 46–47

Ford Employee Scholarships, 159–160

Foreign language study, 270

Free-lunch program, 134–36

Gifted Child, The, quotation from, 62

Gifted children: Big City program, 59, 60–61, 67–69; characteristics of, 64–65; Cooperative Research Program, 66; costs, 254; definition of, 63; and income, 59–60; and intelligence tests, 67–69; Jewish, 66; librarians', 64; segregation of, 63; and social class, 61–62; Soviets and, 58–59; 7

Grades, 82–83

Graduate education, preparation for, 193–94

Grammar, 264–65

Gray, William S., on reading, 31

Great Cities Project, 246

Group memberships, 147

Group projects, 272

Guidance, occupational, 273

Hand, Harold C., on student expenses, 204–205
Handlin, Oscar, on reading materials, 37–38; on teacher attitudes, 231–32
Harvard University, 188
Harvard University admissions committee, on intelligence tests, 63–64
Havighurst, Robert J., on delinquency, 69–70; on school-board membership, 236
Health: elementary school, 99–105; examinations, 102–103; medical treatment, 103–104
Health education failures, 164
High School of Music and Art, 66
Higher Horizons Project, 244, 246
Hollingshead, August B., on Elmtown extracurricular activities, 168–69; on Elmtown high school rewards and punishment, 84–86; on Elmtown intelligence tests, 41
Home, and intelligence, 45–47, 48, 49, 69; and personality, 93–94
Homework, 191–92, 270

Illness drop-outs, 98
Incentives, 279–81
Income: Big City family, 3–4; Detention School family, 72; and educational level, 11–15; and gifted, 59–60; high school family, 154; Negro, 15; and occupation, 12–13; and social class, 10–11, 13; table of Big City groups, 24; Ungraded Class family, 71; white collar, 12
Integration, see Segregation, Negro
Intelligence, native, 8–9
Intelligence tests: and admission to reading improvement programs, 34–35; Big City, 43–44; and college preparation, 190–91; First Grade, 46–47; and gifted, 63, 67–69; and income, 39–40; and motivation, 41; and social class, 42, 43, 51–53; summary of limitations, 52–53; validity of, 40–41, 42, 48–53; 6

Iowa Achievement Test: elementary school scores, 26, 27–30; high school scores, 155, 156–57; 25
IQ, see Intelligence tests

Jewish attitude toward scholarship, 193; gifted children, 66
Johnson, Arthur C., Jr., on delinquency, 75–76

Kahl, Joseph A., college study, 190–192; on social status in grades, 28
Kentucky, University of, reading materials experiment, 36
Krugman, Judith I., on home environment, 93–94; on out-of-school experiences, 145–46

Labor unions and school boards, 235, 236, 237
Librarians and scholarships, 162
Libraries, public, 35, 261
Lipset, Seymour Martin, on English schools, 248–49
Lloyd, Donald J., on English language teaching, 263; on field trips, 260; on intelligence test validity, 47–48
Loeb, Martin B., on middle-class culture, 76–77

McGrath, Earl, on high school drop-outs, 202–203
McWilliams, John T., on reading and delinquency, 262
Marks and grades, 269
Meeting rooms, use of, 167
Meier, Arnold, study of gifted, 62
Method, author's, 23–25
Middle-class culture, 76–79
Milner, Esther, reading readiness study, 31–32
Mitchell, James V., Jr., personality test, 89–93
Montague, Joel B., study of high school drop-outs, 206–207
Moon, Rexford G., Jr., 187
Mooney Problem Check List, 94
Moore, Omar Khayyam, reading experiment, 260–61

Munro, Dean, 187
Murcell, James T., on intelligence tests, 43

National Merit Scholarships, 160–62
National Scholarship Service and Fund for Negro Students, 187
National Scholastic Awards, 160
Negroes, income, 15; and social class, 16
Newspaper influence on schools, 238

Offices, student, 83–84
Ohio Social Acceptance Scale, 83

Packard, Vance, 181
Parent groups: costs, 254; elementary school, 106–12; high school, 165–66; 227–29
Parents, 268
Platoon system, 269–70
Prizes, 83
Promotion: by income groups, 54; problems of, 55–58; 270
Psychological Clinic, Big City, 87–89

Reading achievement scores, 29
Reading: Bereday remedial experiment, 32–33; and home, 32, 34–35; improvement, 33–34, 35, 256–62; and intelligence, 35; materials, 35, 36, 37, 38; significance of, 30–31
Reading Readiness test, 43, 45–46
Recreational facilities, elementary, 143–44; high school, 217
Remedial teachers, 198–99
Rent, 143
Research, Department of Instructional (Big City) testing program, 94
Rheumatic fever, 99–100

Scholarships, 86, 159–61, 187–88
School-Community Behavior Project, 74–75
Secondary Modern schools, 247, 248
Segregation: by ability groups, 194–197; British, 248–49; by gifted, 59, 62; high school, 152, 175–76, 178–179; by intelligence tests, 42–43,

51–53; Negro, 17; race in Big City, 241–42; race in New York City, 243–44; 268
Sex factors in education, 276, 277–279
Sims, V. M., on teacher attitudes, 230
Slocomb, Herline, on gifted, 66
Social studies failures, 163
Soviets, and ability groupings, 199; and gifted, 58–59; and intelligence tests, 50
Sports programs, 272
Special Service schools, 244–45
Status Seekers, The, quotation from. 181
Stouffer, Samuel A., on curriculum segregation, 176; on parental attitudes toward college, 192–93
Strang, Ruth M., on reading, 31
Stuyvesant High School, 66
Summer school, costs, 254; enrollments, 166

Teachers: experienced, 122; men, 275, 279; new, 121; out-of-class aid to students, 85; salaries, 120–121, 254; social attitudes of, 230–234; social origin of, 229; standards for elementary school, 116–117; substitute, 117–20, 211–12, 268; visiting, 255; 267
Teaching machines, 267
Television, 267
Tests: achievement, 25, 26, 27–29, 30, 50, 156, 157; First Grade Intelligence, 46–47; Mitchell personality, 89–94; Reading Readiness, 45; 269; *see also* Intelligence tests
Textbooks: costs of, 206; reading, 35–38; 260, 268, 271
Toby, Jackson, on basic skills, 28
Transportation, elementary school, 115
Tuberculosis, 100–101
Turnover, elementary school, 95–98; high school, 158–59

Ungraded classes, 70, 71, 255

University Freshman Honors Class, 160

Upgrading Program (Big City), 209–210

Vaccinations, 101

Vernon, P. E., on intelligence tests, 48

Visiting Teacher program (Big City), 87, 88–89

Volberding, E., on out-of-school experiences, 146

Ward, Lester, on intelligence, 8–9

Warfel, Harry R., on English language teaching, 263; on field trips, 260; on intelligence tests validity, 47–48

Warner, Lloyd, on Old City ability groups, 196–97

Welles, Sam, report on New York City high school gifted, 66

Who Shall Be Educated? quotation from, 179–80

Witty, Paul, on gifted, 62

Work-load, teacher, 274–75

Work skills achievement scores, 29

Work-study programs, 209–10, 271

Writing, 265–66